RENDER UNTO GOD

RENDER UNTO GOD

A Theology
of Selective Obedience

by

Thomas A. Shannon

PAULIST PRESS
New York / Paramus / Toronto

This book originated as a dissertation submitted in partial fulfillment of the requirements for the degree of Doctor of Philosophy in the Graduate School of Boston University.

Library of Congress
Catalog Card Number: 73-92233

ISBN: 0-8091-1802-5

Published by Paulist Press
Editorial Office: 1865 Broadway, N.Y., N.Y. 10023
Business Office: 400 Sette Drive, Paramus, N.J. 07652

Printed and bound in the
United States of America

Contents

To my wife Cathy
who taught
so I could write.

Prenote

In the writing of this book, the author has received help and support from several people. My thanks go first to my advisors, Dr. Paul K. Deats, Jr., Chairman of the Division of Theological and Religious Studies at Boston University and Dr. Gordon C. Zahn, Professor of Sociology at the University of Massachusetts-Boston. Both of these men extended to me their time, concern and advice, as well as their friendship. Such relations with these men made the original writing of this book both a rewarding academic experience and a sharing of work with colleagues. A special word of thanks goes to Dr. Zahn for writing the introduction to this book. The author would also like to thank James Carroll, the Newman Chaplain at Boston University for his reading of the manuscript and helpful advice about its form and content, as well as for his interest and encouragement.

Special thanks must go to my cousin Charles Schmalz for giving of his time and talent to design the cover of this book. His efforts are greatly appreciated.

I would like to thank in a special way my wife Cathy for continuing her teaching career so that I might be free to work full time on this book. In appreciation for her help and support, I gratefully dedicate this book to her.

Foreword

It is a scant twenty years since I received my first invitation to appear (as part of a 4-man panel) before a general Catholic audience to present my views on conscientious objection and the pacifist implications of Christianity. Not only have these opportunities increased in number over the intervening years, but my role has shifted from that of spokesman for a "lunatic fringe" point of view to that of representative of a recognized and eminently respectable theological position. At the present time, in fact, it is the defender of the older "just war" tradition who is likely to find himself faced with unreceptive, if not openly hostile, audiences. As further evidence of the profound change that has taken place in two short decades, I recently found myself in the quite unexpected position of serving as a designated supporter of the American hierarchy and its official pronouncements against conservative critics who had charged that these episcopal endorsements of selective conscientious objection, amnesty for war resisters, and the like, were leading the Catholic faithful into error.

That such statements are merely reflections—and, I would suggest, relatively timid reflections at that—of the new course set for the Church by Popes John XXIII and Paul VI, as well as the Fathers of Vatican II, is sometimes overlooked. A more significant expression of this new course is to be found in the behavior of a growing number of Catholics all over the world, but especially in the United States, who have chosen to actively reject war and participation in war. Catholic conscientious objectors to American participation in World War II numbered a few hundred at most, a total that has been multiplied several times over in the opposition and open resistance to the war in Indochina. For a Roman Catholic bishop to join clergymen of other faiths in a direct appeal to Air Force chaplains calling upon them to encourage the men in their spiritual charge to refuse bombing orders would have been simply unthinkable a few short years ago. What we have, then, is a record of "selective obedience" in actual practice. Shannon's work is an effort to provide a formal and systematic rationale.

The theory he proposes obviously provides theological support for individual conscientious objection and even for those exhortations to disobedience, but its full significance extends beyond these restricted, and essentially "negative" applications. Instead it revives and develops certain implications of the Christian message which previously unchallenged interpretations and practice have tended to obscure, ignore, or even repress. In this formulation, *obedience* to human authority is no longer to be taken for granted or "presumed" in advance; rather, such obedience will require the same measure of deliberation and moral justification as would a decision to refuse to obey. Nor is this all. Given the order of absolute priority affirmed by the religious community for its own system of values and obligations, each individual believer is charged with the personal responsibility to apply these standards to public policies or programs as they affect his social behavior. Questions of conformity and obedience, under the theory presented here, could no longer be resolved by recourse to a "presumption of justice" which has enabled far too many, far too often, to suspend their consciences or evade making difficult moral decisions and their potentially inconvenient consequences.

This is a particularly propitious moment for the discovery, or rediscovery, of the principle of selective obedience. Until now, as Shannon's historical survey shows, its particular claim to behavioral relevance has been in the area of war and peace concerns. This will undoubtedly continue to be true. If the Indochina war has forced our attention to the gaps and loopholes in the traditional "just war" formulations, its end (when it finally comes!) will provide the opportunity to explore broader and more basic questions relating to the viability or applicability of the tradition itself. National policies which openly contemplate or merely carry the covert threat of "future Vietnams" will come under serious moral review and, when they do, the individual Christian is likely to find himself faced with the choice to cooperate with or resist such policies. If, as seems obvious, some of these "future Vietnams" will be found in Latin America, this would necessarily present a special dimension of trial and ambivalence for American Catholics to the extent that they recognize common religious bonds with the populations subject to the destruction and devastation that might follow.

By the same token, anticipated advances in military weaponry and technology will make it increasingly difficult (if, as I would hold, it is not already impossible) to stretch the concept of the "just means" to cover even conventional war, not to mention the special case of the so-called "ultimate" (i.e., nuclear, chemical, and bacteriological) warfare. The Catholic who would contemplate accepting military service under these circumstances will have to give careful consideration, before he commits himself, to the moral implications of participating in the increasingly depersonalized, even computerized, destruction of large numbers of his fellow human beings. If such a Catholic is at all serious about his Christian commitment and the responsibilities it places upon him, he will have to determine for himself, not only *whether* military service itself can be justified but, assuming he decides it can, the moral limitations he would have to place upon specific acts he might be ordered to perform. We know that thousands of servicemen have already been forced into conscientious desertion by the inhuman and immoral demands of the war in Indochina and uncounted others have faced military sanctions, while remaining in uniform, for protesting specific military policies that violated their moral convictions. These actions, too, find justification under Shannon's theory of selective obedience.

The principle and its application should not be considered however only in the limited context of war and military service. As an ethical principle it is operative in any area of public discourse or social behavior in which the demands of Church and State seem to diverge or threaten to come into conflict. Examples of situations in which it might be applied, or should have been applied, abound. One needs only consider the less than inspiring record of concessions and conformity to racist laws and practices in the American South or to the more subtle manifestations of the same moral evil in our cities of the North. If one can take some pride in the fact that a heroic measure of selective obedience was demonstrated by German Catholicism in its public opposition to the Nazi euthanasia program, one must also confess that it was almost completely lacking with respect to Hitler's patently unjust wars or the infamous "Final Solution."

As Shannon notes, a new issue is emerging which will greatly enhance both the importance and the acceptability of his theory. The same Catholic, whether lay or clergy, who still finds it difficult to comprehend and accept the principle of selective obedience as a basis for refusing military service will have little or no difficulty when it comes to defending the right of medical personnel to refuse to participate in abortions. Even the "radical" notion that one may legitimately refuse to pay taxes for war and the weapons of war is likely to take on an altogether different coloration when the argument is transposed into a refusal to pay taxes that might be used to subsidize abortions or abortion facilities. However much one may regret that this awareness that moral judgments must be made in performing what are generally taken to be the "ordinary" duties of the citizen has been so late in developing, there is reason to hope that the pattern of unquestioning obedience to secular authority is about to be broken once and for all.

This volume should contribute significantly to that end and, in the process, help free the Catholic community from the nationalistic predispositions that have led it into scandal in the past. Whether that scandal be seen in the record of German Catholic support for Hitler's wars or American Catholic support for the war in Vietnam—or in the patriotic declaration by a Massachusetts legislator (ostensibly Catholic!) that the veterans of past wars, like the veterans of the present, "all put COUNTRY before CONSCIENCE"—it can no longer be tolerated in silence in a world faced with the real possibility of nuclear annihilation. Once the principle of selective obedience receives the general recognition it deserves, such statements will still be possible, of course; but it is unlikely that they will stand unchallenged as this apparently was. At the very least, those who would still subscribe to such sentiments will be obliged to come to terms with the fact that the decision to place "country ahead of conscience" and obey can be no less a matter of moral deliberation and judgment than the decision to refuse.

One last note. Some may find a note of impropriety in my accepting this opportunity to write an introduction to a book which bases a considerable part of its argument upon my own past writings and ideas. However, I am fully prepared to leave Dr. Shannon's evaluation of the validity and significance of those works to the judgment of his readers. Therefore, I have restricted these brief comments to my assessment, based on personal life experiences as seen from the sociologist's perspective, of the promise this volume holds for the Catholic Church in formulating an adequate response to the serious challenges that have emerged in the past few years and are sure to be even more demanding in the days that lie ahead.

Gordon C. Zahn

Chapter I
Introduction

A. General Introduction

Since the beginning of Christianity the problem of the relation of the Church to the State has caused many difficulties for both Church officials and civil authorities. One major problem underlying the Church-State issue is which order can make ultimate claims for obedience and loyalty. When both Church and State claim ultimate significance for the lives and values of their members, tension because of the recognized claims of both societies is sure to follow. To focus on some of the issues involved in the vast area of Church-State relations, I will concentrate on one Church, the Roman Catholic Church, and one aspect of this Church's relation to the State: the limits of obedience to the nation-state in American democratic society.

The problem of the Church and its members giving obedience to the State is an important one and has many practical applications—not only in America but elsewhere. For example, in 1945 the Spanish Catholic Church was given official recognition and protection by the Franco regime. And the 1953 Concordat with the Vatican guaranteed Franco the right to nominate residential bishops—in exchange for a clergy salaried by the State, compulsory religious education in all schools and universities, a prohibition of divorce, and a recognition of only religious marriages as legal.[1] This situation presents the problem of the State's control of the Church and the use of the Church

---

[1] Alain Woodrow, "The Candle and the Stick: Post-Conciliar Catholicism: Spain." *Commonweal,* 48, 13 April 1973, pp. 128-131.

as a form of social control to achieve secular ends, namely stability and order.

Also in South American countries, the Catholic hierarchy has traditionally supported the established powers and represents a blending of the sacred and secular. Part of the present ferment in Latin America is being caused by some Church officials, clergy, religious and laity, seeking to break from the *status quo* and have the Church serve as an agent for achieving social justice.

One may also legitimately wonder what the situation in Nazi Germany might have been if the Catholic Church had not sought so hard to achieve a *modus vivendi* with Hitler and his regime. The fear of losing privileges and the majority of its membership helped keep the Church silent in the face of manifest injustice and frequent violations of the natural law.

B. The Church and State in America

The relation of Church and State in America is the result of complex socio-political and religious forces. Although this development is too complex to present fully, nevertheless some aspects can be indicated to show some of the factors which influenced the development of American Catholicism.

1. The Socio-Political Background

American Catholicism was heavily influenced by nationalism—but of an Irish variety. In the period of consolidation, American Catholicism was shaped and directed by an Irish hierarchy—either native born or of immigrant stock—who had already reconciled Irish nationalism with Catholicism. It was an easy matter for them to transfer these nationalistic overtones in their religious practices to America. The precedent for nationalism in religion was there and nationalistic elements in American society made it easy to unite American nationalism and Catholicism.

The nativist movement also led to demanding a reaction of hyper-patriotism on the part of American Catholics. Because the vast majority of Catholics were immigrants, they fell victims to the excesses of nativism and responded by developing strong feelings and practices of patriotism to prove their undying devotion to America.

Related to the nativist movement was the nationalities movement which warned of the danger of immigrants still being controlled by the government of their homeland. Although most American Catholics were not Italians, the pope was perceived as a foreign power who could command the allegiance of the American Catholics. Coupled with this was the persistent rumor of the takeover of America by the Vatican. (At this point it may be instructive to recall some of the debates and issues discussed during John Kennedy's campaign.) Again the reaction of American Catholics was to deny the political dimensions of the papacy and to affirm allegiance to America.[2]

2. The Religious Background

Part of the American Catholic experience was to incorporate elements of the American culture into itself, a very normal sociological process.

One instance of this was a partial democratization of the Church by allowing the trustees of the parish to control the properties of the parish and its funds. Eventually the trustees exercised the right to hire or fire the pastor. In 1850, Pope Pius IX reminded American Catholics that the bishop had control of the diocese and his were the final decisions and ultimate authority in the diocese. American Catholics returned to the traditional practice of the exercise of authority in the parish.[3]

The specter of the heresy of Americanism also shaped the development of American Catholicism. In 1899, Leo XIII is-

---

[2] For a complete analysis of this problem, consult Dorothy Dohen, *Nationalism and American Catholicism* (New York: Sheed and Ward, 1967), especially pp. 175-77.

[3] E. E. Y. Hales, *The Catholic Church and the Modern World* (Garden City, New York: Image Books, 1960), p. 169.

sued the letter *Testem Benevolentiae* to the American bishops. In this letter, Leo condemned several things: (1) to win converts, the Church should adapt itself to the current age with respect to discipline and doctrine; (2) spiritual direction is less necessary than before; (3) the natural virtues are more important than the supernatural ones; (4) the active external life is more important than the passive internal life.[4]

Although Leo never said any American Catholics actually said or practiced these things, the result was the adoption of an attitude of total fidelity to Rome. The American Church found itself in the position of having to prove its Catholicism to Rome. As a result, American Catholicism has placed great emphasis on loyalty to the pope and ecclesiastical authority, the religious discipline of the Church, and strict conformity to external religious practices. Thus the Catholic Church in America gained the reputation of occasionally acting more Catholic than the pope.

This socio-political background has led to a type of dualism in American Catholicism. On the one hand, there is a hyper-patriotism designed to prove the loyalty of the Catholic to the nation-state and on the other hand, there is a hyper-Catholicism designed to prove the loyalty of the Catholic to Rome. This dualism had led to a confusion of where ultimate loyalties lay and to a confusion of the rights of both Church and State over their members. This tension in American Catholicism has, in effect, produced Catholics whose political conscience is shaped by the State and whose religious values are seen as divorced from the realities of life such as social justice, racial justice, and the problem of war. As such, the problem of obedience to the State has tended to be resolved in favor of the civil authority. This book hopes to put a different perspective on these particular issues.

C. Issues in Contemporary American Society

The issue of law and order has become a familiar slogan in American political life. Politicians of varying hues have

---

[4] *Ibid.*, pp. 172ff.

endorsed this cause and many segments of American society have responded to it because of various fears in their own lives. Yet underlying this issue is a certain arrogance toward the law itself. It is more than a using of the law to repress minority groups and perceiving the law as a way of maintaining power. It is the arrogance of going beyond the law to enforce the law. This zeal for what can be described as legal over-kill finds expression in recent statements about the need to reinstate capital punishment and the need to obtain judges who will not be soft on criminals or who will not treat them with pity.[5] This attitude shows up again in the sweeping claims made for executive privilege which indicate a contempt for the legal process. The Rev. Billy Graham expressed this type of arrogance in his retraction of his statement that rapists should be castrated. He said, "It is interesting to note that the thought of castration stirs a far more violent reaction than the idea of rape itself. Perhaps this is part of our permissive society's sickness."[6] But could one not also say that perhaps the reaction was because of the suggested punishment? Rape is a serious crime but one can rightly ask if revenge is to replace punishment. This is not unlike destroying the village in Vietnam to save it.

The problem of the extent of the war-making powers of the executive is also a problem for contemporary America, even though it does not *seem* to be a burning issue now. Yet bombs fall in Cambodia without any justification being given to Congress or citizens. The issue of the creeping omnipotence of the executive is one that needs debate and resolution. It relates very clearly to the law and order issue—by claiming extra-legal sanction for questionable actions—and has serious international consequences.

The abortion issue has raised cries of outrage and protest from many people, especially the Catholic hierarchy and many members of the Catholic Church. It raises the issue of the right

---

[5] For an analysis of the equity of the legal processes, consult Richard Harris, "Annals of Law. I and II." *The New Yorker,* 14 April 1973, pp. 45-88 and 21 April 1973, pp. 44-87. Also see Stewart Alsop, "Our Supererogatory President," *Newsweek,* 9 April 1973, p. 120 for an example of an analysis of arrogance in dealing with the law.

[6] *Time,* 16 April 1973, p. 40.

to life, the definition of life itself and the issue of who can claim the right to make these types of life and death decisions. The abortion issue also raises the problem of the relation of Church and State inasmuch as there is the need to discuss the conscientious right of a doctor, a nurse, or a hospital to refuse to participate in abortion procedures as well as the question of the possibility of conscientiously refusing to pay taxes that are used to support public abortion clinics.

For a variety of reasons, most American Catholics have never dealt with problems such as these. And Roman Catholic theology never seriously confronted issues like these. However, the gradual rise of the so-called New Catholic Left, as well as the pressure of public events, has occasioned public and private discussion of many of these issues. Now individual Catholics and Catholic theology have been faced with events that force the issue, and the old Church-State problem lies just below the surface.

These problems in American society and in the Church need to be addressed by Catholics to clarify the Church and its members' position vis-à-vis social justice, the role of law and the State itself. This is not to be done to find *the* Catholic response, but rather to use the resources of the Church's tradition to evaluate the situation of the country, to judge its actions, and to act so as to ensure the genuine possibility of justice and equality for all.

The problems and questions in this book deal with the relation of ethics and politics, the relation of the Church and State, and with the question of the limits of the political responsibility of the Roman Catholic citizen. They are crucial questions, affecting the welfare of the State and the integrity of the Church. In this book I hope that through an ethical and political analysis I can provide the sorts of criteria and frameworks that people need if they are to be responsible citizens and faithful Christians.

D. Some Limits and Assumptions

The specific problem that this book deals with is that of

selective obedience to the nation-state within the tradition of Roman Catholic social philosophy. I intend to examine this position in both official Catholic documents and theological tradition and commentary. And for purposes of making a more thorough examination of the problem, the main body of the analysis of ethical data will be limited to developments within Roman Catholicism from the reign of Pius XI to the present. As ethical principles emerge, I will test them for general political applicability and relevance by examining them within the framework of a theory of democracy. I will explore: (1) the political responsibilities of the citizen to the nation-state and (2) the limits on loyalty to these political obligations which may be imposed by Roman Catholic social philosophy. As such limits become clear, I will examine them in the light of selected case studies and court decisions. Issues pertaining to the position of selective obedience can be described and conclusions drawn as to the applicability of this position to political life within the nation-state. I will be talking about obedience and disobedience, not merely about political dissent or assent. Under what conditions may the Roman Catholic citizen obey the government? Under what conditions should he or she disobey? That is the twofold question of this book.

My considerations will have three levels of analysis: historical, critical, and constructive and normative. The historical analysis will discuss both official Roman Catholic documents and the theological tradition based on them as developed by Catholic authors. These chapters will deal with the papal teaching from Pius XI to Paul VI and the teaching of Vatican II. The writings of Catholic authors such as Jacques Maritain, John Courtney Murray and Gordon Zahn will be examined to see the interpretation of the teaching and its application to specific situations. There will also be a discussion of the formation of conscience, with an emphasis on the role of obedience. The problem of the relation of the individual to society, especially from the viewpoint of political obligation, will also be discussed in this context. The second level of analysis will be a critical discussion of the political obligations of the citizen in relation to ethical norms as well as obligations arising from membership in a democratic society. This discussion will be continued through an analysis of specific cases which will test the applicability of these ethical norms to the life of the Roman Catholic citizen in the nation-state. The final level of analysis will be constructive and normative. Conclusions concerning the ethical and political responsibility of selective obedience will be formulated to set forth the ethics and politics of selective obedience.[7]

In 1960, Gordon Zahn called for a return to a position that would allow the Christian to give Caesar [the State] his due, but only after the Christian had first conducted an examination that would ensure that what Caesar demanded was really his due.[8] This was the first hint of what can be called a theory of selective obedience to the State. As such, this suggestion of Zahn calls for a reversal of the traditional understanding of obedience in the Roman Catholic understanding of Church-State affairs.[9] This tradition has placed great emphasis on the divine origin of the nature of secular authority, although this authority came to the ruler only indirectly. The emphasis of the tradition was on obedience: the question of dissent was treated as an exception, the practice of which was carefully qualified by both Church authorities and theologians. The obedience due the State was of a rather unqualified nature; only the repetition of the Biblical injunction that we obey God rather

---

[7] Implicit in the book is the use of a methodology developed by J. C. Murray which is significant because it demonstrates the historical conditioning of so-called absolute principles within Catholicism. The methodology has four states. (1) A tracing of the stages of growth in the tradition in its history. (2) Discerning the elements of the tradition that are embodied in historically conditioned situations. (3) Discerning the growing end of the tradition. (4) The formulation of a synthesis that is both old and new. Consult Thomas Love, *John Courtney Murray; Contemporary Church-State Theology* (Garden City, New York: Doubleday and Company, Inc., 1965), p. 219.

[8] Gordon C. Zahn, "Social Science and the Theology of War," in *Morality and Modern Warfare: The State of the Question,* William Nagle, ed. (Baltimore: The Helicon Press, 1960). Reprinted in Gordon Zahn, *War, Conscience, and Dissent* (New York: Hawthorn Books, Inc., 1967), p. 40.

[9] For a summary of the tradition, consult Jerome G. Kerwin, *Catholic Viewpoint on Church and State* (Garden City, New York: Hanover House, 1960).

than man served as a restraint on the Church's articulation of its theory on Church-State relations. The Church, to be sure, retained its own authority and guarded its power; at times, the popes claimed total authority over the emperor in both religious and secular affairs. But as the tradition settled, the Church both recognized and accepted the proper autonomy of the State. With only limited exceptions, the tradition of the Church emphasized that obedience must be rendered to the State; dissent is an exception to this principle.

In terms of the history of this tradition, Zahn is one of the few modern Catholics who have challenged this tradition in a systematic fashion. His suggestion to reexamine the tradition in order to rethink the obedience owed the State has basically not been followed. The late John Courtney Murray, S.J., who did so much to develop contemporary Catholic Church-State theory, accepted the basic Natural Law framework of the Catholic tradition, along with its traditional implications of obedience to the State.[10] Hints of a theory of selective obedience can be found in *Pacem in Terris*[11] of Pope John XXIII and *Dignitas Humanae,*[12] Vatican Council II's statement on religious liberty. These isolated statements refer only to the necessity of the authority's being in conformity to the will of God and the illegitimacy of forcing one to act contrary to his or her beliefs. The theories of political theology, developed by Metz[13] and Schillebeeckx,[14] emphasize the prophetic nature of the Church in the light of a theory of eschatology. Though they do not deal

[10] For an introduction to Murray's work, consult *We Hold These Truths* (Garden City, New York: Doubleday and Co., Inc., 1964). For an examination of Church-State relation, consult "The Issue of Church and State at Vatican Council II," *Theological Studies,* 27 (June, 1966), pp. 580-606.

[11] John XXIII, *Pacem in Terris,* no. 49. Quoted in William J. Gibbons, ed., *Seven Great Encyclicals* (Glen Rock, New Jersey: Paulist Press, 1963), p. 300.

[12] Vatican II, *Dignitas Humanae,* no. 2. Quoted in William A. Butler, *The Documents of Vatican II* (New York: Guild Press, 1966), p. 679.

[13] Johannes B. Metz, *Theology of the World.* Trans. by William Glen-Doepel (New York: Herder and Herder, 1969).

[14] Edward Schillebeeckx, *God, the Future of Man.* Trans. by N.D. Smith (New York: Sheed and Ward, 1968).

specifically with selective obedience, elements of their theories can be used to support such a theory.

The traditional emphasis in Roman Catholic social philosophy has been on the necessity and legitimacy of obedience to the State. Zahn has provided the only constant critique of this framework and has thereby provided several elements of a theory of selective obedience. I hope to take Zahn's suggestion seriously and conduct an examination of the tradition of the Church to work out a consistent theory of selective obedience to the State. Elements from the writings of Zahn and other authors will be reworked into a new synthesis so that an alternative to the traditional model of obedience to the State can be provided that will specify the political obligations of the Catholic who is also a citizen.

Chapter II
Roman Catholicism
and the State:
An Historical Background

A survey of the relations between Roman Catholicism and various nations and states can do no more than indicate some general positions that have been crystallized both through philosophical discussions and wars of religion. There is a complexity of historical, philosophical, and theological data, together with many contributions from nationalism, which have shaped Catholic teaching on this problem over the centuries. Thus this chapter is designed to indicate problems that have arisen and solutions which have been offered, as well as imposed, by the Catholic Church.

One problem in dealing with the history and traditions of the Church in this introductory section is that not all relevant periods of history can be dealt with in depth. Also, the history of the Church is filled with examples which contradict or compromise the theoretical position of the Church on a particular issue. Thus, in the case of the topic of this book, for every example of the Church's obedience to the State that can be given, an example of the Church's disobedience to the State can also be provided. What this indicates is that the practice of the Church was shaped by the concrete historical and political forces of a given period. But along with the practice of the Church, a dominant theory of Church-State relations was being developed, even though in a given period it may not have had a direct relation to the Church's practice. This section provides a brief examination of the statement of this dominant theory of obedience with particular reference to Augustine and Thomas, and, in the modern period, Pope Leo XIII who brought the Thomistic synthesis to a new prominence within the Church. The purpose of this is to sketch out the theory of the Church on its relation to the State as presented by classical theology. From this survey of the problem, we can find a background for the contribution of the 20th century to the problem of selective obedience to the State.

In viewing the classic New Testament texts on Church-State relations, we find different approaches and differing conclusions. Oscar Cullmann, for example, argues that there is a unified New Testament teaching on the State in Matthew, John and Paul which has two propositions: (1) the State is not a definitive order of society, and (2) the State has the right to demand what is necessary for its existence—but no more.[1] Cullmann argues that this position comes from two viewpoints reflected in the Gospels, one seeing Jesus as closely connected with the Zealots and another seeing him set apart from political life.[2]

Heinrich Schlier takes a different viewpoint when he distinguishes between the Lucan-Pauline tradition and the Johannine tradition. Schlier says: "The apostle Paul shares the Lucan view of political authority as an element of order in the face of the destructive powers of the world and his view of the possibility of collaboration between the political authorities and the preachers of the Gospel."[3] The Johannine tradition sees the State as having a legitimate sphere of operation in this world but this position carries with it the danger of neutrality before truth which implies a potential closing off of the world from

---

[1] Oscar Cullmann, *The State in the New Testament* (London: SCM Press, Ltd., 1957), p. 37.

[2] Oscar Cullmann, *Jesus and the Revolutionaries* (New York: Harper and Row, 1970), p. 7.

[3] Heinrich Schlier, *The Relevance of the New Testament* (New York: Herder and Herder, 1968), p. 228. The potential evil of the State is also analyzed in terms of the Book of Revelation which describes the State from an apocalyptic point of view. Here the State closes itself off from truth and does not recognize any derivation of political authority from God's mandate. Hence, the Christian will have nothing to do with the State and will suffer persecution. *Ibid.*, pp. 235-37.

God and acknowledging Caesar as its source of ultimate salvation.[4] Roland Bainton also subscribes to Schlier's understanding of the New Testament view of the State.[5]

Coupled with these differing opinions on the exegesis of the New Testament, we have the historical opinion of Troeltsch who states that Jesus' message had nothing to do with social reform and that he completely ignored the State as well as Jewish nationalism.[6] He also argues that Paul, in contrast to Jesus, "did not merely recognize the State as permitted by God, but prized it as an institution which at least cared for justice, order and external morality."[7] Troeltsch sees a dualism in the New Testament view of the State in that there is both an acquiescence to the existing order as well as an opposition to the State.[8]

The State, because it is a check on evil and an instrument of justice, has a just end which gives it a sacred character. This view, emerging from *Romans* 13, also seems to have a *paraenetic* dimension because it warns Christians not to have the hostile attitude to the State that the Jews had because such hostility would lead to persecution.[9] This also seems to be the case with 1 *Peter* 2: 13-17 which is both a warning not to be hostile to the State and an admonition that the freedom proclaimed in the Gospel is not to be absolutized.[10]

This ambiguity in the New Testament is reflected in the history of the Church by the uses to which the different interpretations and traditions have been put. There are also indications that early in the formation of the New Testament, Paul was borrowing concepts from Stoicism to illustrate points about

---

[4] *Ibid.,* p. 238.

[5] Roland Bainton, *Early Christianity* (Princeton: D. van Nostrand Co., 1960), p. 51.

[6] Ernest Troeltsch, *The Social Teaching of the Christian Churches.* Vol. 1. (New York: Harper Torchbooks, 1960), p. 61.

[7] *Ibid.,* p. 80.

[8] *Ibid.,* p. 148.

[9] Schlier, *op. cit.,* p. 229.

[10] Sir R. W. Carlyle and A. J. Carlyle, *A History of Mediaeval Political Theory in the West.* Vol. 1. (New York: Barnes and Noble, no date, 4th printing), p. 93 and p. 97.

authority which he thought to be important.[11] These concepts have found their way into the Christian tradition. Thus, rather than attempt to defend a particular exegesis, it seems wiser to trace the New Testament teaching on the Church and State through the history of the Church. It is safe to assert that there is an ambiguity in the New Testament with respect to a doctrine of Church-State relations and that the traditions of the Church took advantage of this ambiguity in response to concrete situations.

For example, Justin the Martyr taught that while Christians worship only God and not the emperor, in all other ways they gladly serve the ruler. This was echoed by Theophilus of Antioch who said that the king should be honored and obeyed, for in some sense he receives his authority from God.[12] Irenaeus goes a step further and argues that while government is not natural to the person, it has been divinely instituted as a remedy for sin and therefore the principle of secular authority is a divine principle.[13] It should be noted that this is a Christian version of the Stoic teaching on the State.

Augustine elaborates on Irenaeus' doctrine by insisting that coercive government did not belong to the primitive state of man and that it is not a natural institution. But coercive government is not improper because the conditions proper to human life have been altered by sin and therefore coercive government is necessary as a divinely appointed remedy for sin. It has a legitimate role and respect is due to it.[14] However, Augustine notes that the State is not the widest society to which the individual belongs; the most inclusive society is the society of all persons under the Kingship of God and the laws of this Kingdom govern all persons and all institutions. Kerwin summarizes Augustine's position as follows.

---

[11] Troeltsch, *op. cit.,* p. 148.

[12] Carlyle, *op. cit.,* p. 129. Yet it is important to remember that Justin and quite possibly Irenaeus suffered martyrdom because of their disobedience to the State. This indicates that the theory they proposed had definite limitations.

[13] *Ibid.,* pp. 130-31.

[14] *Ibid.,* pp. 126-28.

If the state commands what contradicts this law, the Christian will not obey. The Christian renders obedience to the temporal authority for the salvation of his soul, but if the pursuance of this end becomes impossible by action of the civil authority, the Christian's obligation of obedience ceases. No man owes absolute obedience to the State. Because of God's law he obeys the civil authority, but in obedience to the same law he may refuse obedience.[15]

Pope Gelasius I (492-97) wrote: "There are two chief powers by which this world is governed, August Emperor: the sacred authority of the prelates and the kingly power."[16] From this perspective, Gelasius set up a model of society which had Christ as head of the Church and the priesthood and the kingship as the heads of the two authorities within the Church. In this model the sacred and secular are dependent and independent. Each is supreme in its own sphere but subordinate in relation to the other sphere. The king looks to the priest for spiritual guidance and the priest obeys the laws of the king whose authority is from the divine order.[17]

One hundred years later, Pope Gregory I stressed even more the authority of the secular ruler. Using the principle that coercive government was a divine remedy for sin, Gregory demanded such respect for the sacredness of temporal power that he condemned as both unlawful and sacrilegious any rebellion against it.[18] Sources for his theory were the Old Testament concept of the position of the king as well as the merger of Church and Empire which occurred after the crowning of Constantine. This position may be summed up with Gregory's statement that, "Those who murmur against the Rulers set over them speak not against a human being, but against Him who disposes all things to divine order."[19] The type of obedience and disobedience described by Augustine finds little support in this position. Yet it is important to remember that Gregory

[15] Jerome G. Kerwin, *Catholic Viewpoint on Church and State* (Garden City, New York: Hanover House, 1960), p. 19.

[16] Quoted in Kerwin, *op. cit.,* p. 19.

[17] Carlyle, *op. cit.,* pp. 190-92.

[18] Kerwin, *op. cit.,* p. 22.

[19] *Loc. cit.*

did not hesitate to contradict his own teaching. In helping to defend Rome against the Lombards, Gregory obeyed neither the Lombard civil rulers nor the Byzantine Roman authorities. He went so far, in this instance, as to sign a truce with the Lombards despite orders to the contrary by the imperial authorities.

This posture of absolute obedience to the civil power was not to remain in the Church for long, however, for a combination of different forces altered the Church teaching substantially. In the 9th century, several events occurred. The doctrine of the Church Fathers began to be stressed and their teachings began to reassert their former authority. The popes had resisted civil authority during the Iconoclast movement.[20] Similarly, in the Teutonic countries a tradition was building which asserted that the king did not possess unlimited authority. Related to this, in the feudal system, was a growing respect for the contractual relation between the ruler and the ruled which implied the fulfillment of mutual duties and a view of authority which was based on a vindication of righteousness.[21]

From an ecclesiastical dimension, the canonists of the 11th and 12th centuries were reemphasizing the power of the pope. These writers of the Church's laws stressed three themes. The pope had, in fact, exercised authority over the appointment and deposition of kings. The pope had exercised authority over both the spiritual and temporal kingdoms—which is indicated by the pope's confirmation of the election of the emperor and the ability to correct him if he misused his authority. Finally the pope could excommunicate an emperor with the implication that his subjects were released from their oath of allegience to

---

[20] The Iconoclast movement began early in the 8th century under the Emperor Leo III. Accustomed to asserting his supremacy in ecclesiastical affairs, Leo forbade religious veneration of images of the saints and ordered the removal of these images from the churches. This set off a series of riots and a counter-attack by the pope. The Iconoclast movement continued for about sixty years and was finally condemned at the Second Council of Nicea in 787. Consult Philip Hughes, *A Popular History of the Catholic Church* (Garden City, New York: Image Books, 1954), pp. 81-82.

[21] Carlyle, Vol. 2, *op. cit.,* p. 32 and p. 74.

him.[22] These lines of development culminated in Gregory VII who attempted to abolish the practice of lay investiture which brought more independence to the Church in running its own affairs. He also stressed that within the Church, kings occupy no different position than other Christians with respect to the observation of divine and canon law.[23] This teaching indicates the possibility of disobedience of the civil authority as well as the Church's having some voice in a definition of secular justice. This line of reasoning was continued by Innocent III who said that while there were indeed differences between the spiritual and temporal authorities, the pope was the one to decide to which category an uncertain matter belonged, a position which also increased the temporal authority of the pope.[24]

With the advent and acceptance of the theories of Thomas Aquinas, the development of the theory of Church-State relations reaches a point of both summation of the past and departure for the future. One new development in Aquinas was that he followed Aristotle instead of the mixture of Platonism and Stoicism popular in the writings of the Church Fathers. Because of this use of Aristotle in setting up his theory of the State, Aquinas did not perceive the State as a conventional institution arising from sinful human nature. Rather the State was a natural expression and embodiment of the moral characteristics of human nature.[25] This implied that government was natural to the person and not a remedy for sin and that its function was to promote human welfare. It followed that the end of government was the attainment of the temporal common good. Within this framework, Aquinas described the authority of the State as coming from God and as having a high purpose—to lead people to a life of virtue. However, there is a higher authority in the world—the spiritual Kingdom of God under the rule of the Pope, the Vicar of Christ, to whom all Christian kings must be subject, as the lower order is to the higher. However, the pope does not hold direct temporal power. There is an indirect

[22] *Ibid.,* pp. 202-13.
[23] Kerwin, *op. cit.,* pp. 25-29.
[24] *Ibid.,* p. 34.
[25] Carlyle, Vol. 5, *op. cit.,* pp. 13-14.

temporal power which the pope may use on certain occasions. He may excommunicate or depose secular rulers if they depart from the faith. Also, the temporal authority must obey the pope in all that is concerned with ordering human life to the heavenly life.[26] Aquinas has several other propositions concerning the duty of the Christian to obey the secular authority. His general principle is that Christians obey secular rulers only insofar as justice requires it and that they are not required to obey any authority which is usurped or which commands unjust things. This defect in the use of authority, as Aquinas calls it, arises when the secular ruler uses his position to command persons to sin or to make them obey in areas to which his authority does not extend.[27] Thus Aquinas distinguishes between secular and spiritual authority but relates them in his hierarchical world view in a way which places limits on the Christian's obedience to the State so that when the Christian does obey, it is to obtain justice and the common good.

Aquinas also briefly deals with the problem of tyrannicide. This problem was introduced by John of Salisbury whose opinion was that a tyrant, one who oppresses the people by violence, has no rights against the people because he has violated the laws and customs of the country and therefore may be justly slain.[28] This solution would obviously be an ultimate act of disobedience against authority. Aquinas approaches the question cautiously. He notes that unless the tyranny is exceptionally grievous, the people should endure it lest matters become worse. Also no private citizen may, on his or her own initiative, accept the responsibility for disposing of a tyrant. The tyrant must be removed by the public authority. The reason for this is that the people have created the king and they can also depose him. Also this act does not constitute sedition because tyranny is not directed to the common good but rather to the private good of the ruler.[29]

---

[26] *Ibid.*, pp. 348-54.

[27] *Ibid.*, p. 91.

[28] Carlyle, Vol. 3, *op. cit.*, pp. 143ff.

[29] Carlyle, Vol. 5, *op. cit.*, p. 32 and p. 96. A partial understanding of the qualification for disobedience to the State is provided by the frequent acts of papal disobedience to the civil rulers which occurred during

Suarez, who developed his theory of tyrannicide during the Counter Reformation, further distinguished two types of tyrants: one who usurps power and a legitimate king who becomes a tyrant. To remove the first tyrant from office by killing him, four conditions must be met: (1) his power must rest on force without consent; (2) there is no recourse possible to a superior authority; (3) the tyranny must be public with no doubt as to its reality; (4) no other means of freeing the community are available. In the second instance of a legitimate king who becomes a tyrant, the community has a certain right to depose him but this must be done by the community, not by a private individual because Suarez argues that insurrection is worse than tyranny and submission is wiser than revolution.[30]

This theory of tyrannicide played a significant part in the history of the English Reformation and was often used out of context. But the doctrine does bear witness to the tradition that civil authority does have limits and that at a certain point obedience may cease and some form of resistance may be a Christian duty. But even here there is hesitation about proclaiming a definite right to be selective in one's obedience, even to unjust authority.

The centuries after the Thomistic snythesis saw many conflicts between Church and State due to the Reformation, the growth of nationalism, and the emergence of new kingdoms and empires as well as the discovery of new continents. Through the conflicts and uncertainties of the period the Roman Catholic Church relied on the principles that Aquinas had developed. Much of the energy of the Church was focused in the direction of safeguarding doctrine and maintaining its authority. The Church entered the political arena with the dual purpose of maintaining purity of doctrine and keeping traditionally Catholic nations both Catholic and doctrinally and politically loyal to the pope. The main period of the formation of theory was over,

---

Aquinas' lifetime, especially in England. The struggle for the Magna Charta, for example, was led by the Archbishop of Canterbury. Moreover, the papacy organized opposition to Frederick II by encouraging the lay lords to disobey him.

[30] Oscar Jaszi and John D. Lewis, *Against the Tyrant* (Glencoe, Ill.: The Free Press, 1957), p. 68.

however, and what followed was an attempt to apply these principles to the new Europe that followed in the wake of the Reformation. The Church in its zeal to proclaim its version of the truth departed from these principles at times. At other times, it would be overanxious to apply them as strictly as possible when it was to its own advantage. These post-Reformation centuries, however, saw no new development of the tradition; the experience, rather, was one of freezing the Thomistic synthesis and striving to maintain conformity to it. This led to a sort of degeneration of the theory in that nothing new was added to it and that few applications of it were made to concrete situations. Historically, the Church became embroiled in many new types of relations with different nations and empires which reflected varying degrees of fidelity or infidelity to its traditions and principles, but from a perspective of a growth of the tradition, very little new was added.

Because of the lack of development of new principles, it is fitting to conclude this chapter with references to Pope Leo XIII who initiated the revival of Thomism and who also helped nudge the Church cautiously into the 20th century. Leo XIII succeeded Pius IX who endured the loss of the Papal States, the *Kulturkampf* in Germany, and harassment of the Church in France. As a result of these concrete situations and his own disillusionment with the liberalism of the day—which was very closely identified with anti-clericalism—Pius IX, from his self-imposed exile within the walls of the Vatican, issued the *Syllabus of Errors,* a list of eighty propositions which could not be held by Catholics.[31] This over-reaction was modified somewhat

---

[31] The *Syllabus of Errors* was a compilation of condemnations gleaned from previous papal pronouncements and listed by Pius IX without reference to the historical circumstances which occasioned these pronouncements. While some of the condemnations were directed at genuine abuses, others were defensive and give the impression of an over-reaction, as the following examples show:

15. Liberum cuique homini est eam amplecti ac profiteri religionem, quam rationis lumine quis ductur veram putaverit.

63. Legitimis principibus oboedientiam detractare, imo ut rebellare licet.

76. Abrogatio civilis imperii, quo Apostolica Sedes potitur ad Ecclesiae libertatem felicitatemque vel maxime conduceret.

by the pontificate of Leo who attempted an intellectual revival in the Church through the Neo-Scholastic movement. One implication of this revival was an attempt to change slightly some of the Church's assumptions about its relations with the world around it.

Leo derives the right to rule from God; political power does not come from the people, though the ruler may be chosen by the people. The determination of who is to rule may be done by the people, but they do not give the ruler his authority.[32] Leo also states that there is a division of power in the world; ecclesiastical, set over divine things, and civil, set over human things. Each is supreme in its own order and each has fixed limits which it cannot trespass. Catholics are bound to love their country but should have a deeper love for the Church because the life within it endures forever. The source of both of these loves is God and because these loves are directed to different spheres, the duties which they imply cannot conflict.[33]

Leo sees a strong need for obedience to the civil authority mainly because the authority of the civil ruler indirectly reflects the authority of God and to resist the former implies resistance to the latter. In one place, Leo maintains that the refusal of obedience to civil authorities can constitute sin.[34] He also says that since obedience to the civil ruler is really obedience to God, no act of sedition may be committed and that the "civil order of the commonwealth should be maintained as sacred."[35] The conclusion drawn is that to cast aside obedience, to incite

---

80. Romanus Pontifex potest ac debet cum progressu cum liberalismo et cum recenti civilate sese reconciliare et componere.
Consult H. Denzinger, *Enchiridion Symbolorum* (Freiburg: Herder and Co., 1937), pp. 483-90.

[32] Leo XIII, *Diuturnum (On Civil Government)*, no. 3. Quoted in Joseph Husslein, ed., *Social Wellsprings*, Vol. 1. (Milwaukee: Bruce Publishing Co., 1940), p. 50.

[33] Leo XIII, *Sapientiae Christianae (Chief Duties of the Christian Citizen)*, no. 3. Quoted in *The Great Encyclical Letters of Leo XIII* (New York: Benziger Bros., 1903), p. 183.

[34] *Diuturnum*, no. 7. From Husslein, *op. cit.*, pp. 52-53.

[35] Leo XIII, *Immortali Dei (Christian Constitution of States*, no. 8. From *The Great Encyclicals, op. cit.*, p. 117.

violence or riots is to commit treason—not only against society but also against God.

But there is another side to the coin of authority and that is divine and natural law. As Leo puts it: "If, therefore, it should happen to any one to be compelled to prefer one or the other, viz., to disregard either the command of God or those of the ruler, he must obey Jesus Christ. . . ."[36] The limit of civil obedience for Leo occurs when the civil authorities overstep their limits and pervert justice by commanding that which is against natural or divine law. In this instance resistance becomes a positive duty and obedience a crime, for if a law is against God it is not a law at all.[37] But resistance is not the first impulse of a Catholic who finds himself or herself in this position; Leo stresses the role of Christian patience, lest through improper actions, society become more disturbed. But when Christian patience and prayer have not brought change and the Christian finds himself or herself obliged to perform an action repugnant to the natural or divine law, then the Christian is told to remember that he or she must obey God rather than man.[38]

Leo revived the basic natural teaching of St. Thomas and put it in summary form for his generation. As before, the theory is clear but the historical precedents show such a confusion of the spheres of Church and State that the theory is difficult to apply and even if cases were clear, there is still a greater presumption of justice on the side of the civil authority than on resistance because authority indirectly mirrors the authority of God.

This historical survey suggests that there is a dominant theory of Church-State relations in Roman Catholicism, that of obedience to the State. This theory is articulated in classical theology by the theoretical positions of Augustine, Aquinas, and the reemphasis given to Thomism in the Neo-Scholastic

---

[36] *Diuturnum,* no. 11. From Husslein, *op. cit.,* p. 55.

[37] *Sapientiae Christianae,* no. 3. From *The Great Encyclicals, op. cit.,* p. 185.

[38] Leo XIII, *Quod Apostolici Muneris (On Socialism ,* no. 7. From *The Great Encyclicals, op. cit.,* p. 28.

period. In particular, the dominant theory of obedience rose to greater predominance following the period of the Counter-Reformation when Church officials bound themselves and the Church to the established order to gain protection from the effects of the Reformation. This involved a strong stand on obedience to the State because the State served as a means of protection for the Church.

Yet, throughout the history of the Church, there have been challenges to this dominant theory by the periodic rise of a theory of dissent, which, however, was normally kept in a position subordinate to the dominant theory. This subordinate theory is especially related to the practice of the Church, particularly in times of crisis. But it did find a place in the classical theory of Aquinas in his development of tyrannicide and was emphasized by Suarez as part of the Counter Reformation movement. But this theory and practice of dissent never gained a position of dominance in the teachings of the Church.

This means that, although the themes of both obedience and dissent are present in the teaching and practice of the Church, the perceived tradition or practice in the Roman Catholic Church as experienced by the majority of its members is that of obedience to the State. This is especially true of the last four centuries. The history of the Church presents, therefore, a dominant position—obedience—and a subordinate position—dissent. In presenting a case for selective obedience to the State in this book, the hope is that the dominant theory can be challenged so that more responsible obedience to the State can be exercised in the light of a theory of political obligation and that the subordinate position can also be challenged to avoid the practice of opportunism by providing an ethical principle which will help evaluate the conditions under which obedience can be given or withheld.

Within the history of the Church-State problem, several models have been rejected by the Catholic Church. Kerwin lists three such models: (1) any model which rejects any distinction between Church and State; (2) any model which implies that any act of the State is legal simply because it was enacted by the State; and (3) any model which says that the

Church and State exist in isolation, having no relationships whatsoever.[39] These are models which have been proposed—and fought over—but they are models which the Catholic Church has rejected from its teaching and has attempted to persuade others from holding.

The traditional teaching that has emerged from this brief survey is best represented by Leo XIII's summary of St. Thomas, the main principles of which are: (1) a hierarchical model of the universe in which the Church is above the State, but in which both have proper ends and spheres of action; (2) the necessity of obedience to the civil authority because this authority comes indirectly from God;[40] (3) a clear implication of a theoretical right to resist unjust authority which is qualified by exhortations to obedience and prayer; and (4) a practical disappearance from the tradition of the theory of permitted tyrannicide. These principles had been formed in a Christian civilization which presumed a clear recognition of what the Catholic Church taught. In effect, they produced a merger of Church and State which collapsed after the Reformation. Though the Church still fought to maintain its absolute claim to truth and the privileges that accompanied it, it also recognized the need for compromise to establish a *modus vivendi* with those in power. Nevertheless, the Church's power was not surrendered without a struggle. This led to a greater fixation on the Thomistic synthesis which allowed some flexibility for the Church. Although the Thomistic model had been

---

[39] Kerwin, *op. cit.*, p. 83.

[40] This represents a preference for what Rommen calls the "translation" model of the origin of political authority. This model states that political authority rests within the body politic as such, although all authority ultimately rests with God. The community, organizing itself into the body politic, holds authority and continues to do so until it is transferred elsewhere. For another to hold authority, it must be transferred to the individual or institution by a free act of the people. Authority comes to the ruler indirectly through the consent of those now subject to this authority. This is distinguished from the "designation" theory which holds that political authority is given immediately by God to a specific individual or institution. This latter theory would leave little room for selective obedience, while the "translation" theory would be compatible with this. Consult Heinrich Rommen, *The State in Catholic Thought* (St. Louis: Herder Book Co., 1945), pp. 428ff, esp. 469-71.

biased in favor of the presumption of justice on the part of the civil authority,[41] there still remains the ultimate reservation that the command of God is to be obeyed rather than that of man.

Throughout its history the Catholic Church has had to come to terms with a variety of forms of governments. In addressing the problem of the obedience of the Catholic citizen to new forms of government, particularly that of democracy, we must ask if the traditional norms, which were formulated in different contexts, can apply to the twentieth century and we must also seek to discover if the Church has provided new answers for the Catholic citizen to use in examining his or her role in participating in new forms of governments. The search for these answers, along with their political and ethical implications, is the task of the remaining chapters of this book.

---

[41] This bias goes back at least as far as Augustine. (Cf. *De Civitate Dei*, I, 26 and *Contra Faustum*, XXII, 75.) Deane indicates that for Augustine it is the monarch alone who has the responsibility of deciding whether another country must be punished for a violation of justice through a declaration of war. Once this has been decided, all must obey his orders, whether they agree with his judgment or not. This soldier is innocent of moral evil in obeying even an unjust command because it is his duty to obey. The citizen also is bound to obey because disobedience would invite anarchy and would throw the State into chaos. Consult Herbert Deane, *The Political and Social Ideas of St. Augustine* (New York: Columbia University Press, 1963), pp. 162ff. For other developments of this bias, see Thomas Aquinas, *Summa Theologica*, II, II, q. 40; Suarez, *De Bello*, VI, third conclusion; and Vitoria, *De Jure Bello*, II, 2.

From a theoretical perspective, this bias can also be related to the theory of Probabilism, a Roman Catholic moral theory used to resolve doubts of conscience. A Catholic may not act with a doubtful conscience; the act in doubt must be either delayed or the doubt must be practically resolved. In this case, if one is forced to act, one may choose the lesser of two evils. This methodology can easily be utilized in the political sphere when enough information may not be available to make a doubt-free decision. Consult Fr. Nicholas Meyer, O.F.M., *Theologica Moralis* (St. Joseph Seminary: *Pro Manuscripto*, 1960), p. 52.

Chapter III
Obedience to the State
in Recent Papal Teaching

The purpose of this chapter is to help lay the theoretical foundation for an examination of the concept of selective obedience to the State. To achieve this purpose, official statements of the teaching magisterium will be examined to determine the official position on obedience to the State. From these statements, conclusions will be drawn relative to the formation of a theory of selective obedience to the State.

A. Pope Pius XI

In the official statements of Pius XI there are three major themes which describe his position on the relation of Church and State: the duty of obedience, nationalism and patriotism, and the role of the Church in politics. In conclusion, a separate analysis of *Mit brennender Sorge (On the Church in Germany)* will be given because this encyclical was directed to the situation of the Church in Nazi Germany and provides a more direct focus to his teaching on obedience to the State.

Pius XI develops the general concept of authority in the tradition of Roman Catholic social philosophy which holds that human authority is rooted in the divine authority of God and more specifically in the office of King which has been given to Jesus Christ. Pius XI emphasizes that Christ's regal office invests the authority of human rulers with religious significance as well as ennobling the citizen's duty of obedience.[1] For this reason, even though the persons who exercise authority within the political community are also inflicted with human frailty and are at times unworthy rulers, subjects will not refuse obedience because they see reflected in human authority the very authority of Christ.[2] The imperfection of human authority makes it even more imperative to recognize that the origin of authority is from God for in this way order and respect for authority will be preserved.[3] On the other hand, the tendency to base authority on man and not on God has brought human society closer to ruin because of the removal or denial of its divine foundation. The formulation of the divine origin of authority carries with it the implication that "man cannot be exempted from his divinely imposed obligation toward civil society, and the representatives of authority have the right to coerce him when he refuses without reason to do his duty.[4]

Along with this obligation to obey, there is also the possibility of disobedience. The right of dissent is given a restrictive definition in terms of a denial of God-given rights which society may not void by making their exercise impossible.[5] Thus we have a condemnation of oaths which proclaim unquestioning obedience and impose obligatory participation in youth groups which are anti-religious.[6] At another point he grants that at times it may be necessary to denounce unjust and degrading human living conditions, but he adds the caution that this be done without giving "any justification for violence under pretext of remedying the evil suffered by the masses, or admitting or encouraging changes in customs deeply rooted in the social

---

[1] Pius XI, *Quas Primas (The Kingship of Christ)*, no. 18, Quoted from Terence P. McLaughlin, ed., *The Church and the Reconstruction of the Modern World* (Garden City, New York: Image Books, 1957), p. 62.

[2] *Ibid.*, no. 18, p. 62.

[3] Pius XI, *Ubi Arcano (The Peace of Christ in the Reign of Christ)*, no. 26. Quoted from McLaughlin, *op. cit.*, p. 37.

[4] Pius XI, *Divini Redemptoris (Atheistic Communism)*, no. 30. Quoted from William J. Gibbons, S.J., ed., *Seven Great Encyclicals* (Glen Rock, New Jersey: Paulist Press, 1963), p. 187.

[5] *Ibid.*, no. 30, p. 187.

[6] Pius XI, *Non abbiamo bisogno (The Apostolate of the Laity)*, no. 61. Quoted from McLaughlin, *op. cit.*, pp. 323-24.

economy,"[7] in order to avoid effecting an evil greater than the one the change was to cure. In the same vein, we have his statement that the "revindication of these rights and liberties can be, according to the circumstances, more or less opportune, more or less energetic."[8] Five principles are offered as guidelines for determining the type and intensity of action as well as who may participate in this action. They are:

1. Revindication has reasons of means or relative ends, not of an ultimate and absolute end.

2. In reasons of means, they must be licit actions and not intrinsically evil.

3. That if they are to be means proportionate to the end, they must be used only in the measure in which they serve to obtain or render possible, in such manner that they do not cause to the community greater damages than those they seek to repair.

4. The use of such means and the exercise of civic and political rights in their fullness, embracing also problems of order purely material and technical, or any violent defense, does not enter in any manner in the task of the clergy or of Catholic Action as such.

5. The clergy must contribute to the prosperity of the nation by encouraging unions of citizens and social classes and collaborating in all social institutions which are not opposed to dogma or the laws of Catholic morality.[9]

These principles lead to several important applications. First, it is not the task of the clergy to participate in the political processes; nor should Catholic Action, a term referring to the incorporation of the laity in the mission of the bishops to spread the Gospel, consider itself as a political party to achieve social goals. Secondly, while the participation of a Catholic in social action is encouraged, it is as a citizen, as an individual Catholic who is exercising his or her civic duties, not specifically religious

---

[7] Pius XI, *Firmissima Constantia (The Religious Situation in Mexico)*, no. 17. Quoted from McLaughlin, *op. cit.*, p. 410.

[8] *Ibid.*, no. 27, p. 414.

[9] *Ibid.*, no. 29, pp. 414-15.

ones. Finally, the common good is established as the highest social value and it is not to be violated in securing the rights of one segment of society. The right of dissent must be seen in the context of the doctrine of the primacy of the common good.

Pius XI also speaks of patriotism, an important virtue because it provides a sense of unity within a given country and is a source of motivation for achieving the goals of the country. This virtue is perceived as a part of Christian charity and this charity controls, sanctifies, and encourages feelings of justified nationalism or patriotism.[10] Pius XI sees this sentiment as leading to deeds of virtue and heroism, but warns that an immoderate nationalism can become the seed of widespread injustice and can lead to a transgression of the norms of justice.[11] Patriotism is a civil as opposed to a religious virtue: "The Church always opposes among its ministers any worldly influences or nationalistic spirit. But above all it opposes these things among those sent in its name to preach the Gospel in foreign lands."[12]

Pius XI develops this apostolic dimension of the Church with reference to the Church's immunity from the power of the State: "Fulfilling the task committed to her by God of teaching, ruling and guiding to eternal bliss those who belong to the kingdom of Christ, she [the Church] cannot be subject to any external power."[13] This is a declaration that the Church's mission is spiritual and thus its accomplishment does not depend on the use of political realities or the power of the State. The renunciation of political ambition or a nationalistic spirit does not totally remove the Church from the political sphere, of course; for if the State should interfere with realities of what the Church considers to be of a higher order, or if it prohibits the Church from accomplishing its mission, the Church has

---

[10] Pius XI, *Caritate Christi (The Present Distress of the Human Race)*, no. 4. Quoted from McLaughlin, *op. cit.*, p. 283.

[11] Pius XI, *Ubi Arcano*, no. 17, *op. cit.*, p. 33.

[12] Lillian Brown-Olf, *Pius XI: Apostle of Peace* (New York: The Macmillan Company, 1938), p. 160. Source of quotation is not given.

[13] Pius XI, *Quas Primas*, no. 30, *op. cit.*, pp. 68-69.

the right to remedy the situation.[14] The divine origin of the Church and its sovereignty in the spiritual kingdom requires freedom and, when this is denied by a lower order, the Church has a prior right for the free exercise of its mission. "When politics draw near the Altar; then religion, the Church, and the Pope who represents them have not only the right but the duty to give indication and guidance which Catholics have the right to request and the duty to follow."[15] Pius XI is affirming that although the Church is not a political reality and does not rely on political means to achieve its ends, having no primary concern for what she terms earthly and purely political affairs, when there is an unjust interference on the part of the State, the Church has the right to reaffirm the proper order of society and to act to secure its rights.

The Church's commitment to these principles as well as the diplomatic skill of the Vatican were soon to be put to the test by the rise of Hitler and the National Socialist Party. Already in 1930, Dr. Meyer, Vicar General of the Diocese of Mainz, issued an instruction which: (1) forbade Catholics to belong to the Nazi Party; (2) did not allow members of the Nazi Party to attend funerals or other Church functions in group formation or in uniform; and (3) forbade administration of the sacraments to Catholics who acknowledged adherence to the teaching of the Nazi Party.[16] The initial strong stand against Nazism, taken by the Catholic Church in Germany, gradually weakened under intense political pressure from the Nazi Party and because of the nationalistic sentiments of many German Catholics, not excluding their bishops, and—once Hitler assumed power—by the Vatican's desire to effect a concordat with the new regime in order to ensure the rights of the Church.[17] The effort to obtain the concordat was directed by Cardinal Pacelli, Pius XI's Secretary of State and the future

---

[14] Pius XI, *Ubi Arcano,* no. 49, *op. cit.,* p. 46.

[15] Brown-Olf, *op. cit.,* pp. 150-51. Source of quotation not cited.

[16] Guenter Lewy, *The Catholic Church and Nazi Germany* (New York: McGraw-Hill, 1964), p. 9.

[17] Gordon C. Zahn, *German Catholics and Hitler's Wars* (New York: Sheed and Ward, 1962), p. 56. These problems are referred to throughout the book.

Pope Pius XII, and he clearly regarded it as a matter of considerable urgency. Pius XI seemed to be less receptive to the idea because of the continued restrictions placed on the Church, especially the official steps taken against the Catholic press, as well as political parties and trade unions whose membership was mainly Catholic and, most troubling of all, the interference with confessional schools and their operations. The dangers Pius XI saw in Nazism led him to issue (14 March 1937) the encyclical *Mit brennender Sorge (On the Church in Germany)*. To avoid the expected reaction, the document was smuggled into Germany, printed in secret, and promulgated primarily by being read from the pulpits.

In his encyclical, Pius XI condemned deification of the State and deification of race as these were forms of idolatry. He condemned forms of education that are anti-Christian and declared it, "the duty of every professing Christian to separate clearly his responsibility from the other side, to keep his conscience clear of any culpable cooperation in such dreadful work and corruption."[18] Obligatory membership in State youth groups was also singled out for censure. Basic to all these criticisms and condemnations was the principle that, "Man as a person possesses rights he holds from God and which any collectivity must protect against denial, suppression or neglect,"[19] and the insistence that human laws which contradict the natural law have a flaw which cannot be corrected by force or power.[20]

It is significant, however, that Nazism as such is not condemned. Indeed there is no serious consideration given to the possibility of disobeying the Nazi regime. Rather the tone is a pained protest, an appeal to the last possibilities, however slight, of a return to fidelity to treaties, and to any arrangement that may be acceptable to the episcopate.[21] Lewy notes that, "While some of Pius's language is sweeping and can be given a wider

---

[18] Pius XI, *Mit brennender Sorge (On the Church in Germany)*, no. 47. Quoted from McLaughlin, *op. cit.*, p. 357.

[19] Pius XI, *Mit brennender Sorge*. Quoted from Anne Fremantle, ed., *The Social Teaching of the Church* (New York: Mentor-Omega Book, 1963), p. 92.

[20] *Ibid.*, p. 92.

[21] *Ibid.*, p. 90.

construction, basically the Pope has condemned neopaganism and the denial of religious freedom—no less and no more."[22] The political implications of Nazism were not considered by the encyclical. Relative to this problem of political authority, Zahn notes that it would be "an exaggeration to regard *Mit brennender Sorge* as a formal condemnation of the Nazi regime by which the German Catholics were released from their obligation of obedience to it as a 'legitimate authority.' Indeed, the encyclical did not even go so far as to terminate Vatican-Reich diplomatic relations."[23] What the encyclical proposes is a condemnation of some extremes of Nazi doctrines, mainly its neopagan character, while omitting direct reference to political and social dimensions of the Nazi regime. The emphasis was on securing religious rights, ostensibly guaranteed under the Constitution, so that the Church could continue its religious services. There was no discussion of the social implications of this posture.[24]

When Pius XI died on February 10, 1939, he left to his successor a war-torn world, a world threatened by totalitarianism and a very difficult religious problem in Germany. Pius XI had enunciated clear principles of Church-State relations; diplomacy and the perceived needs of the Church in concrete situations softened the application of these principles to the real situation. He had recognized the dangers of excessive nationalism and of the State's trying to control the altar, but he was willing to accommodate these principles for what he considered greater good. Despite his many misgivings about the German concordat, he gave his consent because, "We wished to spare

---

[22] Lewy, *op. cit.,* pp. 158-59.

[23] Zahn, *op. cit.,* p. 77, footnote. It is also interesting to note that Hitler was never formally excommunicated from the Catholic Church nor were the doctrines contained in *Mein Kampf* considered dangerous enough to be placed on the Index of Forbidden Books.

[24] One of the main problems that the Church had to face was the reality of Article 32 of the Concordat which stated that the clergy and religious could not be members of political parties or sponsors of political action. This article did not define the term "political." This ambiguity gave the Nazi government a ready means of suppressing any Church activity it did not care for. Consult Lewy, *op. cit.,* p. 84 for a discussion of the Concordat.

the faithful of Germany, as far as it was humanly possible, the trials and difficulties they would have had to face, given the circumstances, had the negotiations fallen through. . . ."[25] This legacy, combining both clear principles and concessions to diplomacy, would now be carried over into the writings and actions of his successor, Cardinal Pacelli.

B. Pope Pius XII

The reign of Pius XII covered three decades filled with the horrors of war, mass exterminations, new scientific discoveries, international efforts at peacemaking, in addition to the daily problems of administering to the needs of the Church. All of these, and many other concerns, were addressed by him in words and actions. In the interest of a systematic presentation, the following categories will be used: some aspects of the Church, the State and their relationship, the teaching on democracy, and his statements bearing upon obedience to the State. Special consideration will be given to Pius XII and Nazi Germany as an illustration of the relation of theory and practice in these areas.

For Pius XII, the Church as a religious entity was founded by Christ as a society that "is visible; and as such meets states in the same territory, embraces in her solicitude the same people, and in many ways and under different aspects makes use of the same means and the same institutions."[26] Within this framework, though, the Church has but one primary mission: to carry the message of the Gospel to all people. This mission implies that the "effect of one or the other political system, however, depends on circumstances and reasons which, considered in themselves, are beyond the scope of the Church's author-

---

[25] Pius XI, *Mit brennender Sorge,* quoted from Fremantle, *op. cit.,* p. 89.

[26] Pius XII, Christmas Message, 1945. Quoted from Vincent Yzermans, ed., *The Major Addresses of Pius XII.* Vol. II. (St. Paul: North Central Publishing Co., 1961), p. 53.

ity."[27] This does not imply that the Church perceives social structures as morally indifferent. Pius XII follows his predecessor in indicating that the Church has the right to judge the moral basis of a social system to see if it is in accord with both natural and divine law.[28] This right is implicit in the fact that one function of the priestly ministry is to give moral instruction to the people, a function which may include giving practical advice on matters of public affairs. Pius XII recognizes that there may be possible abuses of this, but insists nonetheless that the civil authority is not to be the sole judge of this. To allow this would be to put the Church at the mercy of the State and could compromise her moral position. Thus, he refers to the problem in Nazi Germany relative to "political Catholicism" to support his position that the Church must have a voice in political affairs.[29] Even though the Church is seen primarily as a religious reality whose mission is to preach the Gospel, it is also a society which coexists with other social groups and which must at times stand in judgment of them because of its own moral criteria.

Pius XII was quite explicit in his condemnation of what he called State absolutism: "the false principle that the authority of the State is unlimited and . . . appeal to a higher law obliging in conscience is not admitted."[30] The State is not exempt from outside criticism and control and ethical and religious perspectives do play a part in evaluating both the theoretical foundations and the action of the State. Pius XII acknowledged the function of the State as one of, "reviewing, restraining, encouraging all those private initiatives of the citizen which go to make up the national life, as so directing them to a common end."[31]

---

27 Pius XII, Christmas Message, 1940. Quoted in Yzermans, *op. cit.*, Vol. II, p. 35-36.

28 Pius XII, Radio Message, 1 June 1941. Quoted from Yzermans, *op. cit.*, Vol. I, p. 28.

29 Pius XII, Allocution to the Sacred College, 16 March 1946. Quoted in Michael Chinigo, ed., *The Teachings of Pope Pius XII* (London: Methuen and Co., Ltd., 1958), p. 285.

30 Pius XII, Christmas Message, 1945. Quoted from Yzermans, *op. cit.*, Vol. II, p. 84.

31 Pius XII, *Summi Pontificatus,* 20 October 1939. Quoted from *Se-*

This common end, however, is not determined by vote or by the inclination of society; it is rooted in both the concept of perfection natural to the person and the order of creation. Within civil society there are, therefore, natural rights and natural ends of the person to which the policies of the society must be faithful and by which the legal question of society must be judged. The law of the State must conform to or at least not oppose "the absolute order set up by the Creator, and placed in a new light by the Revelation of the Gospel."[32] In his critique of State absolutism, Pius XII reaffirms the traditional natural law definition of the State. *Summi Pontificatus* (20 October 1939), Pius XII's introductory encyclical, stressed the fact that the State is not autonomous, that it is always subject to judgment and correction in the light of natural law. Nothing new is added to the tradition; he merely condemns an extreme theory of the State which had gained widespread acceptance. The traditional natural law doctrine stood in opposition to these excesses, at least on a theoretical basis and it clearly rejected, as Pius XII developed in an address to Catholic lawyers, a complete separation of the Church and State,[33] although in the practical situation the degree of union or separation is a situation often determined by historical circumstances. The overriding concern, however, is that the Church has the freedom to attain its religious mission.

It is in the doctrine of natural law that the Church finds its mode of entry into civil affairs. Because part of the Church's moral teaching is based on natural law philosophy, the Church can correctly say that its sphere of interest is not exclusively religious. Since Church and State both claim, at times, authority over the same subject—the Catholic citizen—the doctrine of natural law offers a way of integrating rights and duties as well as understanding the basis of the Church's indirect right to judge

---

lected Letters and Addresses of Pius XII (London: The Catholic Truth Society, 1949), p. 84.

[32] Pius XII, Christmas Message, 1944. Quoted from Yzermans, *op. cit.,* Vol. II, p. 84.

[33] Pius XII, Address to Fifth Convention of Italian Catholic Lawyers, 6 December 1953. Quoted from Yzermans, *op cit.,* Vol. I, p. 276.

the morality of political discussion.[34] These are problems that pertain to the moral order, to matters of conscience, and to the attainment of man's final end.[35] Church and State, then, are interrelated but not separate. Each has special competence to achieve its goals. But because they are also interrelated, theoretically and existentially, there are areas in which conflict or cooperation becomes possible. The Church, in the doctrine of natural law, provides a theoretical model with which to judge these problems and also serves as the final arbiter of its moral teaching. The Church, as Pius XII develops the argument, claims no competence in political affairs, but it does affirm its right to instruct its members in what it considers to be morally right and wrong.

Yet though Pius XII makes a case for the possibility and occasional necessity of political involvement through issuing moral ultimata, he also shows a great reluctance to use this type of sanction. In 1941, he avoided making a judgment about the Second World War and explained his neutrality in terms of universal charity and the desire to avoid the charge of partisanship. Again in 1942, he refined this by saying there was no need for the Church to take sides over problems of domestic order on international relations as long as the laws of God were being observed, but added to this the assurance that the Church was not renouncing its right to make such statements if necessary.[36] The political neutrality of the Church was based, in addition to the principle of universal charity, on the fact that the Church does not belong to any one group of people and that it is not to be a stranger anywhere. "The Church, which has received from the divine Savior a mandate for all nations to lead them to their eternal salvation, does not intend to inter-

---

[34] Pius XII, Address to Tenth International Congress of Historical Sciences, 7 September 1955. Quoted from Yzermans, *op. cit.,* Vol. I, p. 359.

[35] Some examples of this are: the purpose and limit of temporal authority, the relation of the individual and society, war: its licitness and cooperation in the making of war, the norms of international life. Consult Pius XII, "The Teaching Authority of the Church," 2 November 1954. Quoted from Yzermans, *op. cit.,* Vol. I, p. 279.

[36] Pius XII, Christmas Message, 1942. Quoted from Yzermans, *op. cit.,* Vol. II, p. 52.

vene and take sides in controversies of mere earthly interest."[37]
A further explanation of his position was his intent "to avoid
scrupulously anything that would add to the affliction of the
oppressed peoples."[38] His argument led to a combination of
religious theory and political awareness that produced a weakening of the moral power of the Church in its relations with the
nations involved in the war.

In discussing democratic forms of government, Pius XII
sees two points in their favor: first, the individual is allowed to
express his or her views on the duties and sacrifices imposed
by society and, secondly, no one is compelled to obey without
first being heard.[39] Yet even within this framework, Pius admits
the necessity of a democracy to have the power to command
with real and effective authority. This is an authority which
receives its dignity and sanctioning power by derivation from
the authority of God.[40] A democracy, if it is to succeed, must
also rest upon the individual moral responsibility of its citizens.
One of the civil duties that Pius singles out for special emphasis
is voting. "It is a strict duty for all who have the right, men or
women, to take part in the election. Whoever abstains, especially out of cowardice, commits a grave sin, a moral fault.[41]
For Catholics, voting entails an additional responsibility in that
they are to vote for candidates who will safeguard the rights of
God, the person, the Church, the family, and the laws of morality. Because of the moral dimension of voting, Pius XII said,
"It is therefore for the Church to explain to the faithful the
moral duties which derive from that electoral right."[42] Within

---

[37] Pius XII, Christmas Message, 1946. Quoted from Yzermans, *op. cit.,*
Vol. II, p. 101.

[38] Pius XII, Sacro Bergente Anno, 7 July 1952. Quoted from Chinigo,
op. cit., p. 373.

[39] Pius XII, Christmas Message, 1944. Quoted from Yzermans, *op. cit.,*
Vol. II, p. 80.

[40] *Ibid.,* p. 82.

[41] Pius XII, Address to Delegates of International Conference on Emigration, 17 October 1951. Quoted from Chinigo, *op. cit.,* p. 388. It
should be remembered that these remarks were made against the background of a possible Communist victory in the Italian elections. Nevertheless, the generality of the principle as it stands is inescapable.

[42] Pius XII, Allocution to the Sacred College, 16 March 1946. Quoted
from Chinigo, *op. cit.,* p. 285.

this general framework of the relation of Church and State, the question of the obligation of the citizen to obey the State can be investigated. Pius XII has two traditional postures: (1) political authority—no matter in what form it is expressed—comes from God and therefore should be obeyed;[43] (2) when the laws of God and man conflict, primary allegiance is to be given to God. Together with these two principles, there is also an insistence upon two other conditions: the right of the Church indirectly to make political judgments and the concern for neutrality because of charity. Taken together, these principles create a bias favoring obedience to the State. One further statement, pertaining more specifically to participation in war, which can, if generalized and placed in the context of these principles, seem to form a basis for unquestioning obedience to the State is:

If, therefore, a body representative of the people and a government—both having been chosen by free election—in a moment of extreme danger decides, by legitimate instruments of internal and external policy, on defensive precautions, and carries out the plans which they consider necessary, it does not act immorally. Therefore a Catholic citizen cannot invoke his own conscience in order to refuse to serve and fulfill those duties the law imposes.[44]

---

[43] Pius XII, *Summi Pontificatus.* Quoted from *Selected Letters, op. cit.,* p. 37. It is interesting to note that Pius XII should emphasize this in 1939, the date of the encyclical, in the face of the problem with the Church in Germany. Although this encyclical was not particularly addressed to the German situation, it does reflect the strength of this principle within the tradition, in that it is reiterated in the face of a potentially dangerous situation.

In this encyclical, Pius XII quite probably followed the outline of an encyclical prepared for Pius XI but which was never published. The encyclical, entitled *Humani Generis Unitas (The Unity of the Human Race),* was primarily a strong condemnation of racism and anti-Semitism; but it also strongly condemned totalitarianism and State absolutism. The condemnation of racism was omitted by Pius XII and the condemnation of totalitarian governments was weakened in his encyclicals. For a further analysis of this, consult Gordon Zahn, "The Unpublished Encyclical—An Opportunity Missed," *National Catholic Reporter* (15 December 1972), p. 9. This issue of the *National Catholic Reporter* also has an article on the background of the history of this unpublished encyclical as well as some excerpts from it.

[44] Pius XII, Christmas Message, 1956. Quoted from Yzermans, *op. cit.,*

This statement must be interpreted in the context of Pius XII's frequent discourses on the evil of war and the legitimacy of national self-defense against an unjust aggressor. In the same Christmas message, he declares that: "It is clear that in the present circumstances there can be verified in a nation the situation wherein every effort to avoid war being expended is in vain, war—for effective self-defense and with the hope of a favorable outcome against unjust attack—could not be considered unlawful."[45] In 1954, Pius XII justified strictly defensive atomic, biological and chemical warfare under certain conditions but noted that if such means would "entirely escape from the control of man, its use must be rejected as immoral."[46] This

---

Vol. II, p. 225. This message, it should be noted, stirred a considerable reaction in West Germany where, as part of a political controversy centering upon the reintroduction of military conscription, the question of the rights of conscientious objectors was being debated. The issue had special relevance for Catholics who were seriously divided between support for Adenauer and his Christian Democratic Union and the "Catholics of the Left" who opposed what they regarded as the re-militarization of their country. Two prominent theologians have gained a certain notoriety by testifying before a legislative committee in favor of a provision assuring Catholics of equal claim to recognition as conscientious objectors. The papal message, coming at the height of the controversy, seemed to many to be specifically addressed to the German situation. In fact, one of these theologians—Heinz Fleckenstein, the Rector of the University of Wuerzburg—privately expressed his conviction that the section in question had been written by a German Jesuit advisor to the Pope. Of special significance to this book, however, was Fleckenstein's reaction to the Christmas message: since the Pope had "spoken" in this fashion, he felt he could no longer give public expression to his support for the conscientious objector provision.

As an aftermath to this, Dr. Gordon Zahn, a visiting researcher to whom Fleckenstein's remarks were made, took the occasion of a visit to Rome to visit Gustav Gundlach, the presumed "author" of the passage. To test its applicability to the Nazi situation, Dr. Zahn suggested to Fr. Gundlach that a strict interpretation of Pius XII's words would have made it impossible for a Catholic legitimately to refuse service in Hitler's wars on grounds of conscience. Gundlach indignantly rejected the interpretation, insisting that the Pope did not preclude the individual's obedience to his conscience and, in fact, *could* not do so under the natural law.

The writer is grateful to Dr. Zahn for providing him with this information.

[45] *Ibid.*, p. 225.

[46] Pius XII, Address to 8th Congress of World Medical Association,

statement expanded a practical judgment made a year earlier relative to the participation of a doctor in ABC warfare; at that time Pius stated that when this type of warfare is unjust, the doctor could not participate in it.[47] Obviously the problem with such statements is that they do not resolve the question of who decides whether this type of warfare is just or unjust, or whether it refers only to specific research or does it extend to actual participation in war. Furthermore, one has the problem of deciding how this 1954 statement is to be reconciled with the 1956 statement against invoking one's conscience when legitimate authority has made its decision.

The tension between legitimate authority and the individual conscience found its severest threat in the problem posed by Nazi Germany. Having been Papal Nuncio there for many years, Pius was very familiar with the German situation and, as we have seen, played a significant part in arranging the Concordat between the Vatican and the Third Reich. In addition, he was considered by many—Germans and non-Germans alike—to be pro-German in his personal sympathies. Whether this is true or not, his dealings with Germany provide a valuable case study of the problems outlined in this section.

The crucial source of tension was the Church's refusal to allow itself to be entombed within the sanctuary whereas the Nazi regime was equally dedicated to the elimination of its political influence. The insistence that the Church's teaching embraced all dimensions of life and that the divine law was superior to man-made laws was clearly a threat to the attempt to create a totalitarian order. In the resulting and continuing conflict between Church and State, the Church maintained this principle in theory, though, with a few exceptions, it avoided putting it into practice. As Lewy puts it: "Anxious not to jeopardize their relations with the Nazi regime more than absolutely necessary, the episcopate adhered to certain self-imposed re-

---

30 September 1954. Quoted from Bernard Haering, *The Law of Christ*, Vol. III (Cork, Ireland: The Mercier Press, 1967), p. 132.

[47] Pius XII, Address to the 16th Congress of International Officers of Documentation for Military Medicine, 19 October 1953. Quoted from Yzermans, *op. cit.*, Vol. I, p. 263.

strictions upon the scope of their moral teachings."[48] In its acceptance of Article 32 of the Concordat which forbade membership in political parties or action on their behalf to priests and religions, the Church had effectively surrendered its political power—a surrender that became all the more complete as the Nazis succeeded in imposing ever broadening interpretations of that Article.

Another dimension of this problem was Pius XII's neutrality. In March, 1939, Pius assured the German Ambassador to the Vatican: "It is not the business of the Church to take sides in purely temporal matters and concerns between the various systems and methods that may be considered for mastering the urgent problems of the day."[49] Friedlander offers two interpretations relative to this neutrality: (1) Hitler's political regime was regarded by him as just as acceptable as any other and (2) Pius hoped to achieve through willingness to negotiate what his predecessor had failed to achieve through a policy of firmness.[50] At another point, the pope confided to the newly appointed Lithuanian Minister to the Holy See that his actions were directed at the salvation of souls and not at involvement in temporal controversies and rivalries between States.[51] Still another motive, supplied by Pius XII in a letter to Msgr. Preysing, Archbishop of Berlin (30 April 1943), was his care to avoid reprisals, greater evils and increased threats to pastoral life in Germany. These various motivations imposed restraint and caution upon his speaking to the German situation; he was, in effect, "facing a door that no key could open."[52]

This determination of the pope, combined with strong nationalistic tendencies on the part of the German Catholics, including their bishops, had some interesting ethical consequences. For example, the German soldier was required to take

---

[48] Guenter Lewy, *The Catholic Church and Nazi Germany, op. cit.,* p. 168.

[49] Saul Friedlander, *Pius XII and the Third Reich.* Trans. by Charles Fullmann, (New York: Alfred A. Knopf, 1966), p. 9.

[50] *Ibid.,* p. 10.

[51] *Ibid.,* p. 47.

[52] *Ibid.,* p. 143.

an oath of unconditional obedience to Hitler;[53] the German episcopate allowed Catholics to take this oath because "no oath could obligate a Christian to do anything which violated God's command and law. . . ."[54] A similar moral calculus also enters in terms of *L'Osservatore Romano's* justification of Pius XII's silence in the face of the invasion of Norway by Germany; the pope reportedly said that there were only 2,000 Catholics in Norway and the Holy See, "though condemning the moral aspect of the matter, must take a practical view and bear in mind the 30 million German Catholics."[55] In the same vein, he is reported to have answered a question dealing with his silence on the Jewish question by saying, "Dear friend, do not forget that millions of Catholics serve in the German armies. Shall I bring them into conflicts of conscience?"[56] Further evidence that the role of conscience was being minimized and its duties passed over in consideration of expedience is found in a letter from Cardinal Tisserant to Cardinal Suhard dated 11 June 1940.

Since the beginning of November, I have persistently requested the Holy See to issue an encyclical on the duty of the individual to obey the dictates of conscience, because this is the vital part of Christianity; whereas Islam—which serves as a model for Hitler, thanks to Hess, the son of a Moslem mother—substitutes for the individual conscience the duty to obey blindly the order of the prophet or his successor.

I fear that history may have reason to reproach the Holy See with having pursued a policy of convenience and very little else.[57]

Pius XII, in his encyclicals and addresses, made a case for the supremacy of divine and natural law, the freedom of the

---

[53] The oath is: "I swear by God this holy oath that I shall render unconditional obedience to the Fuehrer of the German Reich and people, Adolph Hitler, the Supreme Commander of the Armed Force, and that as a brave soldier, I shall be prepared at all times to risk my life for this oath." Cf. Lewy, *op. cit.,* p. 239.

[54] Lewy, *op. cit.,* p. 240.

[55] Friedlander, *op. cit.,* p. 52.

[56] Lewy, *op. cit.,* p. 52.

[57] Friedlander, *op. cit.,* pp. 55-56.

Church, and its right to preach the Gospel. In Germany these principles were translated into a theoretical right of the Church to participate fully in the life of the society and not to be restricted to the walls of the church building. In actual practice, however, these principles were not put into practice. The Church's moral power systematically eroded without resistance. Lewy's judgment that "while thousands of anti-Nazis were beaten into pulp in the concentration camps, the Church talked of supporting the moral renewal brought about by the Hitler government,"[58] indicates the extent of the moral failure of the Church, failure that found its limits in concrete form with the execution of millions of Jews, without any institutional protest against this violation of natural law. The German experience reveals a chasm between theory and practice, one that finds its source in a combination of factors: a bias in Catholic theory toward obedience to the authority of the State; an overriding fear that demanding fidelity to principles might provoke opposition; reprisals might give rise to large scale desertion on the part of the faithful from the Church.

C. Pope John XXIII

After the long reign of Pius XII, there was naturally a great deal of interest in the process of selecting the new pope. When John XXIII was finally elected, the entire world was surprised. His advanced age led many to regard him as only an interim caretaker pope; none suspected he would become the best loved as well as the most innovative of modern popes. In his brief reign, John issued two major encyclicals and by calling the ecumenical council, set in motion reforms which are still shaking the foundations of the Catholic Church. This section will concentrate only on *Mater et Magistra (Mother and Teacher)* and *Pacem in Terris (Peace on Earth),* leaving the documents of Vatican II to be discussed separately in the next section.

Mater et Magistra, written on 15 May 1961, picks up the

---

[58] Lewy, *op. cit.,* p. 318.

issues developed in *Rerum Novarum* and *Quadragesimo Anno*. The encyclical deals mainly with economic issues: wages, the role of the laborer and the problems of agriculture—a topic not previously given much development in papal encyclicals. Because of its emphasis on these issues, there is little attention given to politics or the role of the citizen within political affairs beyond the general statement that everyone who is a Christian will, "contribute as far as he can to the advancement of civil institutions."[59] Once again there is the indication that the Church has not only the right to safeguard the principles of religion and morality but also has the right to make authoritative pronouncements on how these principles, which come from the traditional political ethics of the Church, are to be implemented.[60]

The encyclical *Pacem in Terris,* written on 11 April 1963, is remarkable in that it is addressed not only to Catholics but to all persons of good will, a significant departure for a papal encyclical. From the perspective of natural law, the encyclical develops an outline for achieving peace and spells out the relations between individuals, states and world government, providing what Cardinal Suenens was to describe as a formula for peace: "Peace among all peoples requires: Truth as its foundation, justice as its rule, love as its driving force, liberty as its atmosphere."[61] Another main theme of the encyclical is that of order. In his opening sentence Pope John states that peace can be established "only if the order laid down by God be dutifully observed."[62] This theme runs through the entire encyclical, which specifically defines, in natural law terms, the rights and duties of individuals and societies.

Part two of the encyclical is concerned with the relations

---

[59] John XXIII, *Mater et Magistra,* no. 179. Quoted in William J. Gibbons, S.J., ed., *Seven Great Encyclicals* (Paramus, New Jersey: Paulist Press, 1963), p. 256.

[60] *Ibid.,* no. 236, p. 269.

[61] Cardinal Suenens, "Address to the United Nations," 13 May 1963. Quoted from ". . . Therefore Choose Life." Pamphlet from the Center for the Study of Democratic Institutions, 1964, p. 63.

[62] Pope John XXIII, *Pacem in Terris,* no. 1. Quoted from *Seven Great Encyclicals, op. cit.,* p. 289.

between individuals and public authority within individual states as well as their respective rights and duties. It begins with the affirmation that every society needs authority to be both well-ordered and prosperous. The authority of the ruler derives its obligatory force from the moral order of the universe which is, in turn, derived from God who is its source and its end.[63] The authority of states may oblige in conscience only "if their authority is intrinsically related with the authority of God and shares in it."[64] This can be construed as support for the theory of selective obedience to the State in that, for authority to have obligatory power, it must be related to the authority of God.

If, however, the authority should command something which is against the moral order of the universe and therefore against God, these laws and the authority issuing them are not to be obeyed. This is supported, first, by the Scriptural statement that "we must obey God rather than men;"[65] and secondly, by the reasoning of St. Thomas who said that any law that falls short of right reason is a wicked law and therefore is a type of violence.[66] Pope John's stress upon the traditional right of the individual to disobey when commanded by the civil authority to commit sinful actions has two specific applications. If a government does not acknowledge the right of persons or if it violated them, the order of this government lacks juridical force;[67] similarly, if the authority of a civil society uses its power against the moral order, the authority of the government ceases to bind.[68]

Putting the matter broadly, the encyclical emphasizes order within the universe and the duty to shape one's life in accord with this order, but John introduces exceptions to this norm if and when the State authorities choose to issue commands which themselves are not in conformity with the moral order of the universe. The locus for determining the binding power of such

---

[63] *Ibid.,* no. 46, pp. 300ff.

[64] *Ibid.,* no. 49, p. 300.

[65] *Acts of the Apostles,* 5:29.

[66] Consult St. Thomas Aquinas, *Summa Theologica,* Ia-IIae, q. 93, a. 3, ad. 2. Quoted in *Pacem in Terris, op. cit.,* no. 59, p. 300.

[67] John XXIII, *Pacem in Terris,* no. 61, p. 302.

[68] *Ibid.,* no. 83, p. 307.

commands is the conscience of the citizen. Since authority is primarily concerned with moral force, "it follows that civil authority must appeal primarily to the conscience of the individual citizen. . . ."[69] And, as previously noted, authority has this moral force only if related indirectly to the authority of God. This gives a larger role to the conscience of the individual than the past tradition had explicitly indicated. And while not providing a specific methodology by which the individual can decide when he or she is bound to dissent or disobey, the encyclical points to the kinds of circumstances which can be used as models for decision making.

The personal influence of John XXIII did not end with his untimely death from cancer; instead it extended into and throughout Vatican II, the council he convened for the specific purpose of opening windows within the Church. The documents of this council, as we shall see, offer even more explicit support for developing the theory of selective obedience proposed in this book.

D. Vatican II

Vatican II, formally opened on 11 October 1962, set for itself the task of creating a spirit of *aggiornamento* within the Church. It was not to be another Council of Trent, which marked the beginning of the Counter Reformation, but a council of the renewal of the Spirit within the Church, opening the way to a new approach to the contemporary world in a spirit of dialogue.

Part of this renewal took the form of a reformulation of the problem of Church-State relations. While there is reference to and application of the past tradition, Vatican II expanded the context of the problem and indicated a new frame of reference. For Leo XIII, human society was 19th century Europe, religion meant the Roman Catholic Church with its single structure of spiritual authority, paralleling the single structure of temporal

---

[69] *Ibid.,* no. 48, p. 300.

authority of the State. Vatican II moved from this limited West-
ern European perspective to a more universalistic outlook.
Human society now became the family of nations that constitutes the world; religion was discussed in historical and pluralistic terms; and the State was viewed in terms of limited
constitutional government. Leo's viewpoint was retrospective,
a call to reestablish the unity that once existed. Vatican II, on
the other hand, was progressive in that it looked to the future
as the proper locus for the development of new structures, including necessarily new relations between religion and government. In viewing the State as constitutional and limited in its
authority, as a political entity whose purpose is to promote
rights and facilitate the performance of duties, Vatican II in
effect desacrilized the traditional Roman Catholic view of secular authority. The State is no longer the institution that defends
and promotes religion, but rather it is to promote human dignity
and the rights of the person, one of which is religious freedom.
To this extent, Vatican II changed the terms of the problem
from that of Church-State to that of Religion and Government,
which is a subdivision of the general problematic of the relation
of religion and human society This framework recognizes the
independence and autonomy of each order and at the same time
asserts the indirect relation between the two based on values
proper to the human person.[70]

Within this general framework, developed in the documents
Gaudium et Spes (The Church in the Modern World) and
Dignitas Humanae (Declaration on Religious Freedom), the
Council Fathers direct their attention to specific problems related to the secular authority. While noting that authority is
needed lest the community fall into chaos, the Council also
states that the authority must direct the energies of all citizens

---

[70] For a further and more detailed analysis of the new framework of
Vatican II on Church-State relations, consult John C. Murray, "The Issue
of Church and State at Vatican Council II" in Charles P. O'Donnell, ed.,
The Church in the World (Milwaukee: Bruce Publishing Co., 1967),
pp. 35-65. This summary follows the general line of Murray's
analysis and has as its purpose the indication of the new context of the
problem.

to the fulfillment of the common good.[71] Furthermore, the authority of the Government is to be exercised within the limits of morality and on behalf of the "dynamically conceived common good, according to a juridical order enjoying legal status. Where such is the case, citizens are conscience bound to obey."[72] This duty to obey legitimate authority is reiterated in the decree *Apostolicam Actuositatem (Decree on the Apostolate of the Laity)* in the provision that Catholics should be loyal to their country and fulfill their civil obligations. Their opinion will be felt and the civil authority will be encouraged to act in conformity with moral principles and this, in turn, will actualize the common good.[73]

In describing the role of the Church within the human community, the Council repeats the traditional teaching that the Church does not have a specific political, economic or social mission.[74] From the Church's religious mission there arises ". . . the right to pass moral judgments, even on matters touching the political order, whenever basic personal rights or the salvation of souls makes such judgment necessary."[75] One dimension of the Church's religious mission is to protect the transcendent value of the human person and one consequence of the mission is the right and duty to analyze and judge actions which pertain to the rights of persons. This personalistic philosophy is the basis of the Church's indirect social mission. The Council further points out this social mission and dimension of its religious life by stating that there is to be no false separation of professional life and religious life. "The Christian who neglects his temporal duties neglects his duties toward the neighbor and even God and jeopardizes his eternal salvation."[76]

Regarding the specific problem of obedience to the civil government, the Council says:

---

[71] *Gaudium et Spes,* no. 74. Quoted in Walter M. Abbott, S.J., ed., *The Documents of Vatican II* (New York: Guild Press, 1966), p. 284.

[72] *Loc. cit.*

[73] *Apostolicam Actuositatem,* no. 14. Quoted in Abbott, *op. cit.,* p. 505.

[74] *Gaudium et Spes,* no. 42. Quoted in Abbott, *op. cit.,* p. 241.

[75] *Ibid.,* no. 76, p. 289.

[76] *Ibid.,* no. 43, p. 243.

Where public authority oversteps its competence and oppresses the people, these people should nevertheless obey to the extent that the common good demands. Still it is lawful for them to defend their own rights and those of their fellow citizens against any abuse of this authority, provided that in so doing they observe the limits imposed by natural law and the gospel.[77]

Also in the context of a discussion of genocide and the issue of war crimes the Council says:

Therefore, actions which deliberately conflict with these same principles (of natural law), as well as orders commanding such actions, are criminal. Blind obedience cannot excuse those who yield to them.[78]

Coupled with these specific statements is the support of the Council for pacifism[79] and also conscientious objection to war.[80] The support for selective conscientious objection has been an obvious implication of the traditional just war doctrine, even though it has not been emphasized or, until recently, recognized. The support for pacifism, though it is circumscribed and balanced by support for the military, implies a greater emphasis being given to the individual and his or her rights against the civil authority.

These citations from the Council indicate a right of resistance to the Government when morality is ignored or when actions or orders contradict natural law. The specific example given is the "methodological extermination of an entire people, nation or ethnic minority."[81] The problem presented by Vatican II is that while it affirms this specific *right* to resist or disobey the Government, it does not discuss the *duty* to resist, actions which may be justified by the right to resist, or whether this resistance or disobedience may be active.[82] This leaves us with

---

[77] *Ibid.*, no. 74, pp. 284-85.

[78] *Ibid.*, no. 79, p. 292.

[79] *Ibid.*, no. 78, p. 291.

[80] *Ibid.*, no. 79, p. 292.

[81] *Loc. cit.*

[82] Herbert Vorgrimler, ed., *Commentary on the Documents of Vatican II*, Vol. 5. (New York: Herder and Herder, 1969), Oswald Von Neill-Bruening, "Commentary on the Text: Part II, Chapter IV," pp. 319-20.

a general right to selectively obey, but the Council fails to come to terms with the implications of the issue.

Related to this right of selective obedience, at least in crisis situations, is an interesting omission from the final text of *Gaudium et Spes.* The Council departed from the common tradition of the Roman Catholic Church when it omitted the sentence—"When there is no evident violation of the divine law, the presumption is that the competent authority is right and its orders must be obeyed"[83]—from *Schema XIII,* the draft presented at the opening of the final session of the Council. As our previous examination has shown, the presumption of justice in the case of doubt is a traditional principle of Roman Catholic political ethics and while its omission does not necessarily imply its rejection, it is most significant that the Council chose not to reiterate it. This intentional omission takes on even greater significance when coupled with the Council's statement, quoted above, explicitly rejecting blind obedience as a virtue.

Vatican II provides us with a new conceptual framework, though not in a finished form, for defining the relation between Religion and Government. This framework continues to stress the value of obedience to the Government but now this is coupled with the strong warning that the civil Government can overstep its juridical limits. While in no way lessening the commitment to the common good, there is a recognition, by clear implication, of a right of resistance, though this right is not extended to a duty nor are the ethical dimensions of this position presented in any detail.

E. Paul VI

The papacy of Paul VI began during the Council and has been influenced by it ever since. Many of Paul's statements have been directed to the renewal of the structures of the Church and the implementation of the various internal reforms of Vatican II. Yet Paul VI has not ignored the world; he is the

---

[83] *Ibid.,* Willem J. Schuijt, "History of the Text: Part II, Chapter V," p. 337.

first pope to have traveled outside the Vatican during his reign; he has repeatedly addressed himself to the issue of world peace. The issue of Church reform and discipline, however, seems to be the focal point of Paul's reign. The major social issues he has addressed are birth control and development, especially as it relates to social, economic, industrial and agricultural theories and programs. His writings seem to presuppose the norms of Vatican II without going into specific detail on the means to implement them. Because of this situation, the writings and speeches of Paul VI do not contribute too much to the topic of this book.

The encyclical *Progressio Populorum (The Development of Peoples,* 26 March 1967) provides the only direct reference to the problematic of obedience to the State. The encyclical discusses the problems of development with emphasis on conditions which make living in dignity difficult, if not impossible. Because the temptation to violence is great in situations like these, Paul gives a principle of interpretation which bears upon the problem of obedience to the State.

We know, however, that a revolutionary uprising—save where there is manifest, long-standing tyranny which would do great damage to fundamental personal rights and dangerous harm to the common good of the country—produces new injustices, throws more elements out of balance and brings on new disasters. A real evil should not be fought against at the cost of greater misery.[84]

In agreement with Vatican II, Paul VI endorses obedience to the Government to the extent that the common good demands, but adds the specific reason for disobeying civil authority: damage to personal rights and harm to the common good. These reasons, along with genocide, provide three instances when the citizen has the right to disobey. Like the Council, Paul does not expand on the duty to disobey or provide guidelines for such decision-making beyond making it explicit that this type of disobedience is to be regarded as an exception, an action to

[84] Paul VI, *Progressio Populorum,* no. 31. (Boston: Daughters of St. Paul, 1967), pp. 19-20.

be taken only when the Government has proven by its actions that it is no longer the legitimate authority. This statement, too, goes no further than the other official statements examined in this chapter; it affirms a principle but avoids dealing with its application or with the ethical dimensions of the consequences of the application of the principle of limited obedience to the State. Paul does not expand the initial steps taken by Vatican II; indeed, it may be suggested that his lack of attention to an issue such as this may suggest a reluctance to deal with a problem that governments may find too threatening. Of course, it may just be that Paul VI sees the internal needs of the Church as the more important problem and therefore has chosen to concentrate his efforts in meeting them. Whatever the reason, one must note the failure to take seriously the concrete moral dimensions facing the citizen who is obliged in conscience to limit his or her obedience to the Government, but is given no guidelines other than proportionality for applying these principles.

F. Summary

This review of papal teaching has indicated several common themes. One, stressed especially by Pius XI and Pius XII, is that of secular or human authority's being a reflection of the authority of God. This is a reaffirmation of a tradition which reaches back to the early centuries of the Church. These popes stressed another ancient tradition: when the laws of God and man conflict, the laws of God are to be observed. In practice, however, these popes emphasized the first tradition, while maintaining the second one primarily in theory. Pius XI and Pius XII do affirm a social mission of the Church which emphasized that Catholics participating in civic affairs do so as private citizens, reserving to the official Church the right to judge the morality of social systems. In addition, Pius XII condemned state absolutism by insisting that the State was not exempt from criticism from an ethical or religious perspective.

Although he set forth many new directions in his brief

reign, John XXIII continued to use the language and categories of natural law as his basis for his social programs. His emphasis, especially in *Pacem in Terris,* was on the use of the natural law in defending and elaborating personal and social rights and duties. Although John agreed with the theory of the indirect divine authority of the secular ruler, he qualified this by insisting that secular authority obliges only when it is in harmony with divine authority. This shift in emphasis implies the necessity of an evaluation of secular authority as well as the possibility of a degree of selectivity in the obedience which must be given to secular authority. This is given specific explication in John XXIII's affirmation that if the Government does not acknowledge the rights of persons or if it violates them, or if the Government uses its power against the moral order, then it is not to be obeyed. This specification indicates a selectivity in obedience to the State not found in the other official documents discussed here.

Vatican II carried the programs of John XXIII forward, especially in the document *Gaudium et Spes.* One important development was that the State is no longer the institution that is to defend the Church, as previous teaching would have it. Instead, the function of the State is to defend and promote human dignity. This grants the State a greater degree of autonomy from the Church and also serves to weaken the indirect divine authority of the secular ruler. Because of this there is a shift to an acceptance of contract theory without, however, accepting an individualistic notion of political authority. Very significant in *Gaudium et Spes* is the deliberate omission of the presumption of justice theory, which was an important part of Roman Catholic social philosophy, as well as a firm rejection of blind obedience as a virtue. This reenforces selectivity in obedience in its clear implication of a duty to evaluate the policy of a Government before obeying. This is especially true because a rejection of blind obedience places more responsibility on the individual to make moral evaluations of the action of the State.

Paul VI, although not addressing himself at length to problems of political theory, stresses that dissent is allowed when there is grave damage to personal rights and harm to the common good. He does note, however, that the Government is to be obeyed to the extent that the common good allows.

Thus, the official pronouncements of popes and the Council have hinted at new directions by insisting on the unity of secular and divine authority as the basis for the obligation of obedience to be incurred and through the omission of the presumption of justice theory coupled with a rejection of blind obedience. However, the emphasis of the tradition is still upon legitimate dissent, not legitimate obedience, as this book would have it. Also, there remains the problem of applying these formulations to a democratic society. These issues will be dealt with in the following chapters.

Chapter IV
Obedience and Conscience: A Commentary and Analysis

The examination of official Church documents has revealed an emphasis on the duty of obedience to the State. Dissent is treated as an occasional phenomenon which is subject to strict regulations. There are strong hints, however, of a theory of selective obedience to the State. This chapter will examine how the question of obedience is analyzed by Catholic authors from different perspectives. Jacques Maritain is selected because of his understanding of the Roman Catholic tradition and his neo-Thomistic synthesis. John Courtney Murray is treated here because of his development of Church-State theory, especially as it relates to American democratic society. Gordon Zahn provides a critique of the traditional Church-State theory and proposes an alternative position. This analysis of these authors, together with an examination of the virtue of obedience and the role of conscience, will provide the immediate context for formulating a doctrine of selective obedience to the State.

A. Developments in Contemporary Authors

1. Jacques Maritain

Jacques Maritain, a French Catholic layman and philosopher, represents a flowering of the neo-scholastic movement in Europe. While searching for answers to personal problems as a young man, Maritain was introduced to Catholicism by Leon

Bloy. Following his conversion, Maritain devoted much time to a study of the philosophy of St. Thomas, whose philosophy still forms the core and heart of Maritain's thought and methodology. It is from this perspective of neo-Thomism and its understanding of natural law[1] that Maritain formulates his doctrine of Church-State relations and the problem of obedience to civil authorities.

Maritain presents an overall view of the structures to which the person belongs and relates the political institutions to this framework. The widest grouping to which the person belongs is the community, which is a product of instinct and heredity in given circumstances or historical frameworks. The community is a response of human nature to a given environment.[2] Within this primal community, society arises as a work of human reason, as a result of the community aiming at a certain end.[3] The nation, which is not yet a political reality is a "community of people aware of themselves as history has made them."[4] The nation is not limited to blood ties or language groups, but is a broader concept reflecting the common past of a group of communities.

To describe the phenomenon of order within society, Maritain distinguishes between the body politic and the State. Political society or the body politic, a requirement of nature and an achievement of reason, is "a heritage of accepted and unquestionable structures, fixed customs. . . . It is, further, common inherited experience and the moral and intellectual instincts which constitute a kind of empirical, practical wisdom."[5]

The State is that part of the body politic "concerned with the maintenance of law, the promotion of the common welfare

---

[1] Maritain defines natural law as follows: "This means that there is, by virtue of human nature, an order or a disposition which human reason can discover and according to which the human will must act in order to attune itself to the necessary ends of the human being." Jacques Maritain, *The Rights of Man and Natural Law* (London: The Centenary Press, 1944), p. 35.

[2] Jacques Maritain, *Man and the State* (Chicago: University of Chicago Press, 1951), pp. 2-3.

[3] *Ibid.*, p. 4.

[4] *Ibid.*, pp. 5-6.

[5] *Ibid.*, pp. 8-10.

and public order, and the administration of public affairs."[6] The State is one aspect of the body politic which specializes in the interests of the whole, the common good. The authority that the State receives comes from the people. For this reason, the State has no natural right to supreme power, but always remains at the service of the common good of the larger political society.

Also of importance in this context is Maritain's distinction between power and authority. Power is defined as the *"force, which one can use, and with the aid of which one can oblige others to listen or obey."*[7] On the other hand, he sees authority as the *"right to direct and command, to be listened to or obeyed by others."*[8]

When Maritain speaks of the Church in his writings, he refers only to the Roman Catholic Church. Maritain accepts the basic tradition of the superiority of the Church over the body politic and the State. And because the Church is within the body politic, there is reason for and the necessity of co-operation between Church and State.[9] Maritain describes the human person, who is a member of both the body politic and the Church, as the locus for this interaction. There is an insistence that the State not be seen as the secular arm of the Church[10] and that "Christianity and the Christian faith can neither be made subservient to democracy as a philosophy of human and political life nor to any political form whatsoever."[11]

Maritain's basic claim for the Church is that it should be free to teach, preach and worship.[12] But in addition to this religious freedom, the Church also has a "right of authority over the political or temporal itself, not because of political

---

[6] *Ibid.,* p. 12.

[7] Jacques Maritain, *Scholasticism and Politics.* Trans. by Mortimer J. Adler. (New York: The Macmillan Co., no date), p. 92.

[8] *Ibid.,* p. 92.

[9] Maritain, *Man and the State, op. cit.,* pp. 152-54.

[10] *Ibid.,* p. 161.

[11] Jacques Maritain, *Christianity and Democracy.* Trans. by Doris C. Anson. (New York: Charles Scribner's Sons, 1944), p. 36.

[12] Jacques Maritain, *The Things That Are Not Caesar's.* Trans. by J. F. Scanlan. (London: Sheed and Ward, 1940), p. 152.

things, but because of the spiritual principle involved."[13] This right is derived from the "two-sword" theory. Maritain says that the sword of the State is under the sword of the Church. The State is "not to be oppressed in its own sphere, but is to be controlled and directed by the upper sword as regards the latter's [the Church] own interest."[14] The Church therefore has an indirect power over the State, particularly with regard to spiritual matters. This power pertains also to the political sphere, as is evident from Maritain's opinion that we commit a "fault against obedience, a fault against the justice and the filial piety which binds us to the Church in resisting an order given by the Church in virtue of her *indirect power over the temporal.*"[15] No specific examples are given, but the implication is that the Church has the right to give commands which bind in conscience in the temporal order by virtue of its indirect authority over this sphere. This authority is also exemplified by Maritain's saying that when it is a question of considering the political activity morally permitted to the Christian, "it is to the Church of Christ to give these rules and these precepts and to particularize them according to the case, I say to the teaching Church, and without anyone—cleric or layman—having authority to increase them of his own right."[16]

Because of this, the Catholic as Catholic and member of the universal Church is above and outside of any political party. But as citizen, the Catholic may support any party useful to the common good which has not been condemned by the Church.[17]

The political obligation of the individual Catholic citizen does not end with the possession of the Christian faith and docility to its ministers. Maritain here cites a need for political experience, examination of facts and positive and critical judgments.[18] Within this theory of political obligation, Maritain also reminds the reader that civil authority has the right to command

---

[13] *Ibid.*, p. 12.

[14] *Ibid.*, p. 12.

[15] *Ibid.*, p. 29. Emphasis in the original.

[16] Jacques Maritain, *Integral Humanism.* Trans. by Joseph W. Evans. (New York: Charles Scribner's Sons, 1968), p. 263.

[17] Maritain, *The Things That Are Not Caesar's, op. cit.*, p. 66.

[18] Maritain, *Christianity and Democracy, op. cit.*, pp. 62-63.

and that the citizen has the duty to obey, even to obey a tyrannical government as long as it is not practically ascertained that insurrection will not result in greater evil to the community.[19] Also Maritain cautions citizens to remember that there is "normally a presumption of right in favor of the superior. . . ."[20] And because of the human tendency to avoid obligation, Maritain stresses that a "precise theory of obedience ought to define the obligations below which, in default of a more generous virtue, it is strictly imperative to go."[21]

Yet within this description of the obligation to obey the State, Maritain sees exceptions. Following his teacher, St. Thomas, he says resistance is possible in two instances: when the people subvert the common good and when sinful acts are ordered to be performed. Again the caution is given that except for these exceptional acts, "by the very fact that civil authority derives from God, men are bound in conscience to obey the laws of the state."[22]

When resistance must be offered, especially when performed by those Maritain describes as "prophetic shock-minorities,"[23] certain norms must still be followed. We must remember that such recourse to resistance is an exception and illegal authority is to be tolerated—as a lesser evil—only when there is a tyrannical government. Secondly, though the use of force may be needed, justice must also hold sway. And finally the people must confirm the outcome through their free approval or disapproval.[24]

Maritain reflects the traditional ecclesiastical teaching on Church-State relations and the obligations the citizen has to obey the civil authority. The duty of resistance is exceptional. He does affirm that political action must be preceded by experience, thought and critical judgment. Nonetheless, these characteristics of Christian political action do not deny the presumption of right on the part of the Government. Selective

[19] Maritain, *Scholasticism and Politics, op. cit.,* p. 105.
[20] Maritain, *The Things That Are Not Caesar's, op. cit.,* p. 50.
[21] *Ibid.,* p. 30.
[22] *Ibid.,* p. 48.
[23] Maritain, *Man and the State, op. cit.,* p. 143.
[24] *Ibid.,* pp. 144-45.

obedience to the Government operates, within Maritain's framework, as an exception and is negatively described as an act of dissent.

2. John Courtney Murray, S.J.

The late John Courtney Murray, while professor of dogmatic theology at Woodstock Seminary, worked out a new and progressive theory of Church-State relations. Murray restudied the traditional teachings of the Church, with special emphasis on the synthesis of Leo XIII, and reformulated the tradition within the context of modern democratic societies, particularly with reference to American constitutional democracy. Since the basic growth of Murray's doctrine on Church-State relations has been examined in detail elsewhere,[25] this section will highlight aspects of his reformulation and will concentrate on his analysis of the problem of selective conscientious objection as this relates to this book.

In his reconstruction of the problem of Church and State, Murray discovered three trans-temporal principles which govern the discussion of Church and State. The first of these is an affirmation of the freedom of the Church: as a Christian people, the membership has the freedom to follow the doctrine of the Church and to obey her laws. Secondly, there is a necessary harmony between the two laws by which the person is governed and between the complex of social institutions and the requirements of Christian conscience. This principle is based on the nature of the person and his or her life in two orders: the sacred and the secular. Finally, there is to be a necessary cooperation of Church and State, a cooperation that is ordered and bilateral.[26] These principles free Murray from seeing any one historical period as having a definitive solution to the prob-

---

[25] Consult Thomas Love, *John Courtney Murray: Contemporary Church-State Theory* (Garden City, New York: Doubleday and Co., Inc., 1956).

[26] Consult Love, *op. cit.*, pp. 146ff for a complete discussion of these principles.

lem of the relation of Church and State. Instead he reasons to general principles which have been continually reapplied during the life of the Church. Murray's synthesis leads to greater flexibility in Church-State relations, stresses the need for continual reapplication of the principles in changing historical situations, and most importantly, recognized the changing character of the State. It is this last point that led Murray to the conclusion that the teaching of one generation may not necessarily be applied to the problems of another.

The political context of Murray's discussion is also important for in it he updates the terminology of the Church in political matters. Murray, following the basic plan of Maritain, speaks of civil society, political society, and the State. Civil society, the widest category, is the "total complex of organized human relationships on the temporal plane."[27] Within this context, political society is the civil society as organized for the common good, constituted as such by effective ordination to the good of the body as such.[28] The State is not the body politic —and here the closeness to Maritain's thought is evident—but the "particular subsidiary function of the body politic, whose special function regards the good of the whole. . . . It is a rational force employed by the body politic in the service of itself as a body."[29] Following this, Murray sees Government as a relation of the ruler to the ruled and vice versa; Government is thus not the State nor the laws.[30] This analysis helps clarify the secular and functional nature of the State within Roman Catholic social philosophy. This autonomy of the State is further exemplified by Murray when he says, "the imperatives of political and social morality derive from the inherent order of political and social reality itself."[31]

---

[27] John Courtney Murray, S.J., "The Problem of a State Religion," *Theological Studies* XII (June, 1951), p. 158, note a.

[28] *Ibid.,* p. 158, note b.

[29] *Ibid.,* p. 158, note c.

[30] *Ibid.,* p. 158, note d.

[31] John Courtney Murray, S.J., *We Hold These Truths* (Garden City, New York: Image Books, 1964), p. 272. It should be noted that Murray argues that the impact of Christian values on political processes comes through their influence on persons engaged in these processes. Cf. *Ibid.,* p. 275.

The concept of the proper autonomy of the State and its right to make and enforce its political decisions are further described in Murray's discussion of selective conscientious objection to war. This discussion also indicates the *prima facie* obligation of the citizen to obey the decisions of the Government. Murray bases this obligation of obedience on what he describes as the "conscience of the laws."[32] This implies a recognition of the "authority of the political community by established political processes to make decisions about the course of its actions in history. . . ."[33] When this process has been followed and a decision made, "at least a preliminary measure of internal authority must be conceded by the citizen to this decision, even by those citizens who dissent from it."[34] This is why the presumption stands for the justice of the decision of the political community. This does not imply that the citizen surrenders his or her conscience to the State, but it is a recognition that the State too has a conscience which informs its laws and decisions. The citizen, therefore, is to concede the justice of the decision until he or she is sure in his or her own mind that the decision is unjust and is able to present a convincing demonstration of why this is so. If the individual's conscience clashes with that of the State, his or her judgment is valid and must be followed; in doing this, the individual still stands within the community and is subject to its judgments.[35] The moral universe within which the decisions must be argued and made comes from the political ends of the State: justice, freedom, security, the general welfare, and peace.[36] These ends constitute the conscience of the laws and the morality of decisions made by the political community must be judged in the light ot them. This means that the individual conscience does not have an absolute right for this would be pure individualism and a denial of the nature of the political

---

[32] John Courtney Murray, S.J., "War and Conscience." Quoted in James Finn, ed., *A Conflict of Loyalties* (New York: Pegasus, 1968), p. 27.

[33] *Ibid.*, p. 26.

[34] *Ibid.*, p. 27.

[35] *Ibid.*, p. 27

[36] Murray, *We Hold These Truths, op. cit.*, p. 272.

community. Yet the political community is bound to respect individual conscience. The existence of this right is correlative to the duty of forming and informing the private conscience.[37]

The thrust of Murray's thought validates the autonomy of the State and the recognition of its authority by the citizen as well as the citizen's giving the presumption of justice to the decisions and policies of the State. In this way, for Murray, there is room for limited dissent to the conscience of the State which is based on the claims of a mature conscience. "Strictly on grounds of moral argument, the right conscientiously to object to participation in a particular war is incontestable."[38] This selective right of dissent applies to all military decisions, which Murray views as a species of political decisions which are made within the context of the conscience of the laws. On the basis of his understanding of the natural law as applied to the political sphere, Murray argues for a *prima facie* obligation of obedience to the State with a limited, selective right of dissent on the part of the private citizen.

3. Gordon C. Zahn

In addition to the personal witness to religious pacifism, Gordon Zahn has also given academic support to the ethical and sociological dimensions of this commitment in books and articles dealing with the problem of the relation of the State and the demands of the Christian conscience. In these writings, Zahn has produced a critique of the traditional articulation of Church-State relations, especially in relation to the presumption of justice on the part of the State, and in its place has proposed a new posture for the Church and the individual Christian in their dealings with the power of the State.

Already in 1960, Zahn raised the issue of the presumption of justice given to the State. He said, "I submit that this formulation requires a thorough re-examination of its adequacy to our times. . . . The new interpretation could require that Caesar first prove the legitimacy of this claim to the Christian's serv-

---

[37] Murray, "War and Conscience," *op. cit.*, p. 30.
[38] *Ibid.*, p. 25.

ice."[39] Some reasons presented for the necessity of this reinter-
pretation are an aggressively jealous nationalism, liberalism in
philosophy, economics and politics, the disunity of Christians,
the errors of rationalism and scientism. These factors coalesced
to produce an un-Christian and anti-Christian atmosphere. For
now *"there is no longer any justifiable basis for assuming that
the demands of the secular ruler or his intentions will meet
even the minimal standards of Christian morality."*[40] Further
weight is given to this position, in Zahn's estimation, by the
new weapons of war and the politics of deterrence. Zahn argues,
from the context of the just war position, that the new weapon
systems and the politics accompanying them create a situation
in which it is impossible to meet the criteria of the just war
theory. Therefore, the burden for the proof of the justice of its
cause must rest on the State, not on the citizen who would
question or seek to deny it.

Implicit in this argument is a critique of the use of authority
by the State and the role of the Church in society. Zahn does
not deny that the State has authority or that this authority
comes indirectly from God. He does argue that this authority
has been abused and that this authority has had, at times,
disastrous effects, e.g., saturation bombing, the slaughter of the
Jews in Nazi Germany and the development of nuclear weapons and politics. Because of what Zahn sees as minimal or
nonexistent considerations of Christian moral teaching in the
decrees of secular governments,[41] he demands that this authority
be challenged by Christian moral standards.[42]

---

[39] Gordon Zahn, "Social Science and the Theology of War," in William J. Nagle, ed., *Morality and Modern War: The State of the Question*
(Baltimore: Helicon Press, 1960). Reprinted in Gordon Zahn, *War, Conscience, and Dissent* (New York: Hawthorn Books, Inc., 1967), pp.
41-42.

[40] *Ibid.*, p. 41. Emphasis in the original.

[41] A recent example of this is provided by Dr. Arthur Schlesinger, Jr.
who said, "If moral principles have only limited application to foreign
policy, then we are forced to the conclusion that decisions in foreign
affairs must generally be taken on other than moralistic grounds." "The
Necessary Amorality of Foreign Affairs," *Harpers Magazine,* August,
1971, p. 76.

[42] Gordon Zahn, "Religion and War," *Newman Review,* Spring 1963.
Reprinted in Zahn, *War, Conscience, and Dissent, op. cit.,* p. 84.

What has happened, however, is that over the centuries, a comfortable *modus vivendi* developed between Church and State. Zahn sees the Church as having become "little more than an agency for channeling or reinforcing the controls of the State in those matters it, the State, defines as crucial to its well-being."[43] Because of this policy, the Church generally tends to be most vocal when it deals with the moral problems of the individual such as sex, financial contributions, and pornography; but the "spokesmen of the Church are likely to be much more inclined to a policy of expedient silence when it comes to passing open judgments upon the actions he is commanded to perform by the state."[44] This vacuum of moral analysis assures the faithful that the cause of the State is just and therefore their obedience is viewed as meritorious and any evil which may be involved will be charged against the one giving the command.[45]

This critique of the Roman Catholic Church, which applies as well to Protestantism and Judaism, as a "vehicle of conformity to the mores and supporters of the secular *status quo*"[46] leads Zahn to his analysis of the role of the Church and the individual Christian within society.

This analysis is controlled by the desire to see the Church return to its earliest traditions which found the Christian "ready to follow the Master's advice to give Caesar his due, but, at the same time, required that he first make sure that what was demanded of him was really Caesar's due."[47] This is a call to return to the Church of the Martyrs, to a Church willing to dissent from prevailing secular values which compromise or contradict Christian values. By holding firm to its orientation to the supernatural order, the Church will be faithful to its

---

[43] Gordon Zahn, "The Case for Christian Dissent," in Thomas Merton, ed., *Breakthrough to Peace: Twelve Views on the Threat of Thermonuclear Extermination* (New York: New Directions, 1962). Reprinted in Zahn, *War, Conscience, and Dissent, op. cit.,* p. 259.

[44] *Loc. cit.*

[45] Gordon Zahn, "The Private Conscience and Legitimate Authority," in the *New Blackfriars,* January, 1966. Reprinted in Zahn, *War, Conscience and Dissent, op. cit.,* p. 133. An earlier version of this essay was published in *Commonweal,* 30 March 1962.

[46] Zahn, "Religion and War," *op. cit.,* p. 81.

[47] Zahn, "Social Science and the Theology of War," *op. cit.,* p. 40.

calling and will not be reduced to the status of just another channel of secular authority.[48] The Church, in this view, is to serve as a form of social control, but the values and the behavior to be controlled are to be in conformity to the end and purpose of the life which the Church incarnates. Zahn sees the Church as one of the few value-forming institutions that is in a position to encourage rethinking of national values and goals as well as national politics. The Church provides this service by proposing values and by being a community of support.[49] In addition to being a center for alternate values, the Church must also serve as a judge of the nation and its rulers and their policies. In doing this, the Church must on the one hand insist upon conformity to moral principles that cannot be compromised and on the other hand it must evaluate national policy in the light of these principles.[50] Sociologically, Zahn describes this role of the Church as the Church-type performing as the sect-type. The Church is forced to act, at times, as a sect because it is committed to a value system that can contradict the values and goals of the State. Because of this value commitment, the Church may occasionally need to find itself as a locus of dissent or rebellion. In terms of this opposition to secular values, Zahn is of the opinion that the Church can and, at times, must operate as a sect because of the threat to its values and the possible loss of salvation for its members which would come from conformity with national or secular values or goals.[51]

This evaluation places a greater responsibility on the individual for moral decision-making. This responsibility comes from a twofold source. On the one hand, the greater the democratic structure of the Government, the more responsible the citizen is for acts of the Government. On the other hand, the greater the commitment to religious values, the more one is

---

[48] Gordon Zahn, *In Solitary Witness* (New York: Holt, Rinehart and Winston, 1964), p. 240.

[49] Gordon Zahn, "The Church as a Source of Dissent," in *Continuum*, Summer, 1963. Reprinted in Zahn, *War, Conscience, and Dissent, op. cit.*, pp. 280ff.

[50] Gordon Zahn, "Afterword: Summation and Prospectus." In Zahn, *War, Conscience, and Dissent, op. cit.*, p. 302.

[51] Zahn, *In Solitary Witness, op. cit.*, p. 203

called to judge all of one's actions in the light of these values, as well as acting on these decisions.[52] Zahn recognizes that this emphasis on the individual has been neglected. He says that the tendency to distrust the moral judgment of the individual is related to an exaggerated notion of the competence of the secular authority.[53] Another reason for this that can be extrapolated from Zahn's writings is the relation of the ecclesiastical authority and the vested interest it has in maintaining good relations with the secular *status quo*. A final reason Zahn gives for the distrust of the individual is a lack of information in the area of where the decision is to be made. Traditionally, a Catholic may not act with a doubtful conscience. Therefore, especially relative to the problem of national policy, it is easy for authority—either Church or State—to say that there are gaps in the individual's knowledge and that a fully informed moral decision cannot be made and that therefore the presumption of justice must be given to the State and its rulers because they know more than the citizens. This resolution of doubt tends to favor conformity to national policy. Zahn comments that to say one is to resolve such doubts in favor of legitimate authority (especially in the case of war) is to "guarantee the unending repetition of that scandal which has always led to brothers in Christ killing one another in the firm conviction that they were fulfilling a Christian obligation in doing so.[54] In addition, Zahn argues that one has to take into account here the effect of propaganda, the suppression of factual information, and false information being supplied to the citizens. These factors do not take away the responsibility for the individual citizen to make moral decisions on the policies of his or her Government. The decisions must be made on the basis of the information available. Zahn comments that a wrong moral judgment of the individual which occurs because the authorities have blocked access to facts constitutes the only case in which the moral responsibility for his actions must be assigned to his superiors.[55]

[52] *Ibid.*, p. 202

[53] Zahn, "The Case for Christian Dissent," *op. cit.*, p. 255.

[54] *Ibid.*, p. 257.

[55] Zahn, "Private Conscience and Legitimate Authority," *op. cit.*, p. 137.

The problem that Zahn sees in Church-State relations is that *"to the extent that the Church does accommodate itself to a secular regime, it becomes, in effect, an agent of that regime, supplementing the secular controls with those of the supernatural order."*[56] To counteract this possibility, Zahn proposes that the Church and its members as individuals detach themselves from both temporal interests and the obligations of the national State. Secondly, a greater emphasis must be placed on fortitude, while the virtue of prudence must be de-emphasized, especially when overemphasis on prudence leads to a weakening of religious values and compromises moral principles. Thirdly, the ascetic ideal of the early Church must be reawakened. This will lead to a reemphasis of the possibility of martyrdom or imprisonment, possible consequences of dissent and nonconformity.[57] This implies that the Church will have to act as a sect and its obedience or conformity to the values and the policies of secular society and the nation-state must be selective.

In terms of individual behavior, Zahn calls for a reaffirmation of faith in the individual to make correct moral decisions and to act on these decisions regardless of the personal consequences.[58] This implies individual acts of dissent and rebellion by the individual in the name of the values of the religious community of which he or she is a member. This clearly implies again the possibility of selective obedience to the State. Zahn's position calls for absolute fidelity to the teachings embodied in the religious institution with the consequence that allegiance can be given to secular institutions only after serious examination and when there is no danger of compromising the primary religious values. It also implies that the natural order needs correction by the religious sphere or the supernatural order. In this way the autonomy of the secular is weakened and the primacy returns to the spiritual. The position Zahn articulates

---

[56] Gordan Zahn, *German Catholics and Hitler's Wars* (New York: Sheed and Ward, 1962), p. 216. Emphasis in the original.

[57] Zahn, "The Case for Christian Dissent," *op. cit.*, p. 261.

[58] Zahn, "Private Conscience and Legitimate Authority," *op. cit.*, p. 138.

and calls for as general practice for the Church and its members is that of selective obedience to the nation-state.

The position that Zahn presents stresses the prophetic or sectarian dimension of the Church. This treatment does not imply a rejection of the Church as an institution acting in harmony with the larger society. Rather it indicates that at times, and especially in times of crisis, a segment of the Church may arise to witness to a value or truth that is in danger of being negated or suppressed by the Church or State. In this way, the prophetic or sectarian dimension serves, in Zahn's analysis, as a corrective to the institutions of Church and State. The prophetic witness is directed to recalling the Church, first of all, to its own values and traditions; it hopes, in the second place, to influence public policy through emphasis on the significance of the value in question as well as through the weight of its arguments. The sectarian dimension in Zahn's analysis should not be perceived as a surrender to radical individualism, but rather as an act of witness destined to recall the Church to fidelity to its values and traditions. This sectarian aspect, therefore, is not a denial of authority within the Church; it is to serve as a prophetic correction to failures of the Church or its leadership to secure its rights and to live out its values. Through this dialectic of Church and sect, Zahn sees the possibility of the Church's retaining fidelity to its mission of proclaiming and living the Gospel.

B. Obedience and Authority

1. Traditional Analysis

Catholic morality has centered around the person as located in a world that is ordered and intelligible. The proper growth of the person and the achievement of his or her personal goals comes from the discovery of this moral order and conformity to it. Because of this, conscience can be broadly defined as the extension or application of natural law to a particular act. Aquinas confirms this by saying that conscience is not a faculty, but an activity: the application of moral science to conduct.[59] Conscience is not the source of morality nor a faculty which constructs a moral standard. It is a judgment of the practical (as opposed to the speculative) reason, based on knowledge, coming from both awareness of the basic principles of natural law and training in moral development, on the conformity or nonconformity of a particular act with the standards of the natural law. This judgment of conscience is binding because it tells the individual what the law is for him or her at this time and in this situation. Aquinas indicates the moral power of this judgment by saying that "Every judgment of conscience, be it right or wrong, be it about things evil in themselves or morally indifferent, is obligatory, in such wise that he who acts against his conscience always sins."[60] Because of this, conscience becomes the ultimate subjective norm of morality in that it is to appropriate the objective norms of the natural law to this particular act of the person. Therefore it is the individual person who bears the responsibility for the act or omission. Yet, to say that conscience is the ultimate *subjective* norm of morality is not to say that it cannot err or that this particular act or refusal to act cannot, in fact, be morally wrong.[61]

One shift in the tradition, which introduced the problem of legalism, was the voluntaryism of William of Ockham and the development of this by Francis Suarez. The insight offered here was that the will was a completely autonomous power and indifferent as to its object. The will then becomes regulated by law, an external principle which obliges and restrains the will. Aquinas' insight that the will is ordered by nature to the good presented by reason and that the regulation of the will comes from within through conformity to the natural good of the created order is weakened and its power in the tradition is deemphasized. The two major consequences of this are that law

---

[59] Thomas Aquinas, *Summa Theologica,* Ia. 1xxix, 13. Quoted in Thomas Gilby, ed., *St. Thomas Aquinas: Philosophical Texts* (New York: Oxford University Press, 1960), p. 291.

[60] Thomas Aquinas, III *Quodlibet* 27. Quoted in Gilby, *op. cit.,* p. 291.

[61] Conscience is to be judged by the *objective* norms of morality, i.e., the will of God or the natural law. For a further discussion, consult p. 80.

as an ordinance of reason now becomes law as an arbitrary restraint and that obedience replaces prudence as the main virtue since an act is now wrong because it is forbidden rather than its not being in conformity with the order of nature.[62]

While this emphasis of Ockham did not completely replace the Thomistic tradition, it did put greater stress on the problem of the correct knowledge of the law within Catholic tradition. In this way, morality came to be identified not so much with conformity to the natural law—though this remains the basis of Catholic morality—but rather with conformity to the prescriptions of moral and canon law and the opinions of the teachers of moral theology. This emphasis is indicated by the descriptions of conscience in the traditional manuals of moral thology.[63] The emphasis on conformity to specific precepts is shown by describing conscience as certain, probable or doubtful insofar as one is in possession of knowledge of the law. Also conscience is described as true or false by reason of conformity to the law in question.

While conscience has not, in the Catholic tradition, lost its role as the ultimate subjective norm of morality and while it is still seen as a judgment of reason on the correctness of this particular act, the context in which conscience has been discussed has changed in that the concept of law was transformed from reason's apprehension of the natural moral order of the universe to the external command of the lawgiver. This led, in turn, to the role of conscience being limited to knowledge of a system of laws and the application of the law to specific cases.

---

62 Joseph V. Dolan, S.J., "Conscience in the Catholic Theological Tradition." Quoted in William C. Bier, S.J., ed., *Conscience: Its Freedom and Limitations* (New York: Fordham University Press, 1971), p. 14.

63 For a sample of the traditional Catholic approach to conscience, consult E. Genicot, S.J., *Institutiones Theologiae Moralis* (Bruge, Desclee De Brower, 17th ed., 1951), pp. 41ff. Genicot defines conscience as "...dictamen rationis seu judicium de liceitate vel illiceitate instantis meae operationis," (p. 41) which is a reflection of the Thomistic tradition on the meaning of conscience. The rest of the tract deals with the problem of obtaining knowledge of the law and what to do when this knowledge is not certain. Absent is a section on the development or formation of conscience.

2. Contemporary Developments

This emphasis on law as a source and motive of morality led to some dissatisfaction among moral theologians. The German moral theologians John Michael Sailer and John Baptist Hirsher were early pioneers who tried to move moral theology away from casuistry to a restatement of the Christian ideal and its relation to the Gospel. Otto Shilling continued this tradition by making divine love the formal principle of moral theology.[64] None of these men denied the laws of the Church, but rather they sought to reaffirm the purpose of moral theology and to allow the warmth of the Gospel and Christian love to permeate what had become a cold, legalistic approach to Christian living.

The person who has inherited these traditions and has worked them, together with traditional morality, into a new synthesis is Bernard Haering in his work *The Law of Christ*. Haering returns to the Gospel as the basis for his theology and describes the moral task of the person as one of responding with a generous and open heart to the invitation of God for union with him through the person of Christ.

In doing this, Haering describes conscience as the "spiritual instinct for self-preservation arising from the urge for complete unity and harmony. The soul craves this inner unity with herself, which is possible only through unity with the world of the true and the good."[65] Haering further says that conscience is to move the will in accordance with the truth of which it is aware and to search for the truth prior to its decision.[66] In this way, conscience makes us participants in the eternal law of God which reveals our likeness to God.[67] By these statements, Haering retains a traditional orientation, but shifts the focus of both conscience and moral theology to the whole of Chris-

---

[64] For a survey of reform movements in moral theology, consult Bernard Haering, C.SS.R., *The Law of Christ*, Vol. 1. Trans. by Edwin G. Kaiser, C.PP.S. (Westminster, Md.: The Newman Press, 1966), pp. 20-33.

[65] *Ibid.*, p. 143.

[66] *Ibid.*, p. 148.

[67] *Ibid.*, p. 147.

tian life, rather than to restricting it to the legal aspect.

In terms of the formation of conscience, Haering steps out of the narrow confines of the legal tradition. Throughout his first volume, Haering lists several factors which must be taken into account in forming a correct moral decision. A partial listing includes: Holy Scripture, the ultimate objective norm— God and the created order, the infallible magisterium of the Church, zeal for truth and a cultivation of the knowledge and value of law, a docility to the Holy Spirit, humility with a sense of sorrow and a purpose of amendment, and the authority of teachers within the Church.[68] The valuable contribution of Haering is that he broadens the realm of areas that inform the conscience. In doing this, he helped prepare the way for the discussion of Vatican II on conscience.

Conscience was discussed in Vatican II primarily in reference to the problem of religious freedom, but several statements about conscience itself were made. Conscience is the mediator through which the person perceives and acknowledges the imperatives of divine law. "Conscience is the most secret core and sanctuary of a man. There he is alone with God, whose voice echoes in his depths. In a wonderful manner conscience reveals that law which is fulfilled by love of God and neighbor."[69] The Council also noted that conscience unites the Christian in the search for truth with the community of humanity and helps the community arrive at solutions to problems. Also the person is bound in all activities to follow the dictates of conscience so that he or she may come to union with God. The Council recognized that conscience may err, mainly from ignorance, but it also emphasized that error does not make conscience lose its dignity.[70]

The Council reiterated the tradition that there is an objective norm of morality to which the individual should conform and that conscience is the subjective norm of morality, even if in error.[71] It also provided guidelines for the exercise of freedom

---

[68] *Ibid.,* pp. 149 through 188.

[69] *Gaudium et Spes,* no. 16. Quoted in Abbott, *op. cit.,* p. 213.

[70] *Ibid.,* no. 14., p. 214.

[71] Richard J. Regan, S.J., "Conscience in the Documents of Vatican II." Quoted in Bier, *op. cit.,* p. 35.

of religion which also serve as models for the formation of conscience as well as indicating some limits. The Council said that in the exercise of all freedoms, the moral principles of personal and social responsibility are to be followed. Persons are bound by "the moral law to have respect for both the rights of others and for their own duties toward others and for the common welfare of all. Men are to deal with their fellows in justice and civility."[72] Society has the right to defend itself against possible abuses done on the pretext of freedom of religion. The Council charges those who have the task of educating others to teach respect for the moral order and obedience to law. Educators are to form persons who will come to "decisions on their own judgments and in the light of truth, govern their activities with a sense of responsibility, and strive after what is true and right, willing always to join with others in cooperative efforts."[73] The Council reaffirms the core of the traditional teaching on conscience, giving emphasis to the fact that while error may make a judgment of conscience wrong, error does not make conscience lose its dignity. Also stressed are the social implications of conscience and its responsibilities in the social order.

In making moral evaluations, it is important to remember that conscience is to be tested and judged by the ultimate objective norm of morality—the will of God which is made known through revelation and the natural law. In effect, revelation serves as the means of illuminating uncertain areas of natural law; in turn, this clarification of natural law specifies the content of revelation. Conscience finds itself, therefore, in tension with this dialectic between revelation and natural law for conscience must always search and weigh evidence, examine the tradition, as well as evaluate new data or perspectives on revelation and natural law before a judgment is made. This dialectic provides the opening for this contemporary analysis which gives conscience a role which includes more than responsibility for the knowledge of canon law. It should be noted, however, that an infallible statement would provide an ultimate

---

[72] *Dignitas Humanae*, no. 7. Quoted in Abbott, *op. cit.,* p. 686.
[73] *Ibid.,* no. 8, p. 687.

norm for judging an issue. This writer knows of no statement in moral theology which has been defined as infallible. Many actions are absolutely forbidden, e.g., a direct abortion, but this is not because of an infallible pronouncement. Therefore, in the normal course of events conscience will be forced to enter into a dialectic of competing values and various sources and levels of understanding and the moral evaluation will have to be made on the basis of the evidence at hand.

3. The Role of Obedience

a. *Obedience to the Church*

Because the Church has traditionally been experienced as an hierarchically structured community, authority has been vested primarily in the pope. Vatican II related the authority of the bishops to that of the pope through the teaching on collegiality, the unity of the pope and bishops in governing and teaching the Church.

In speaking of the bishops, Vatican II stated that "Episcopal consecration, together with the office of sanctifying, also confers the office of teaching and governing."[74] When the teaching is in communion with the pope, the bishops are to be respected as witnesses to Catholic truth, and in matters of faith and morals, they speak in the name of Christ and the faithful are to "accept their teaching and adhere to it with a religious assent of soul."[75]

Within this context of the bishop's authority, Vatican II presents three major motives for obedience to the bishop: (1) the motive of unity in Christian life; (2) the imitation of the obedience of Christ; (3) the authority conferred by Christ on the bishops who are the successors to the apostles. This last reason is based on both a precise intervention of God in history which gave the Christian community a hierarchy with power to

---

[74] *Lumen Gentium (Dogmatic Constitution on the Church)*, no. 21. Quoted in Abbott, *op. cit.*, p. 41.

[75] *Ibid.*, no. 25, p. 48.

govern and on the spiritual gift of the Holy Spirit given to the bishops to perform their tasks.[76] Two other motives offered as a basis for obedience are founded on love for the common good. Obedience is necessary because no one individual can decide what the common good is and also because ultimate authority rests with the bishops in union with the pope, the head of the Episcopal college, and order demands respect for obedience.[77]

Vatican II also made special note of Papal infallibility in matters of faith and morals. The Council noted that "religious submission of will and mind must be shown in a special way to the authentic teaching authority of the Roman Pontiff, even when he is not speaking *ex cathedra*."[78] When the Roman Pontiff (or the College of Bishops speaking with him) defines a judgment as an article of faith, he pronounces it in accord with Revelation and all are obliged both to hold and be ruled by this declaration.[79] Even when a revealed truth is not defined in such a manner, the faithful are to be attentive to the words of the pope and to follow his mind which can be known from his documents, his frequent repetitions of the same doctrine, or from his manner of speaking.

The styles of exercising authority within the Church together with the corresponding obligation of obedience can be schematized in the following way, after the manner of Carlo Cardinal Colombo.

1. The teaching of the individual Bishop in communion with the Pope. This is an official witness to divine truth and must be listened to with reverence by all.

2. The authoritative teaching of a Bishop in his own diocese. This teaching or doctrinal decision must be listened to with religious respect.

---

[76] Joseph Lecuyer, C.SS.P., "Obedience to the Bishop." Quoted in Karl Rahner, S.J., ed., *Obedience and the Church* (Washington, D.C.: Corpus Books, 1968), pp. 65-67.

[77] *Ibid.*, p. 69.

[78] *Lumen Gentium*, no. 25. Quoted in Abbott, *op. cit.*, p. 48.

[79] *Ibid.*, no. 25, p. 49.

3. The authoritative teaching of the Pope which is not *ex cathedra*. A deeper religious assent of will and mind in proportion to the degree of the authority involved.

4. The authoritative *ex cathedra* pronouncement of the Pope. This requires absolute religious consent.[80]

These statements reflect the traditional description of hierarchical authority within the Roman Catholic Church. The emphasis, even with the doctrine of collegiality, is on the hierarchy as the teachers and the faithful as the ones who obey their authentic and authoritative teaching.[81]

Within recent years, especially after the promulgation of the encyclical *Humanae Vitae (On Human Life)* of Paul VI, the question of what type of obedience must be given to authoritative, non-infallible teachings of the hierarchy has been publicly raised without, however, challenging the concept of infallibility. Charles Curran writes that the question of error in non-infallible papal teaching had been discussed in early 19th and 20th century theology. He also notes that conservative opinion within the Church indicated a right to dissent from the authority of encyclicals; this situation occurred because of disagreement concerning the content of Pope John XXIII's encyclical *Mater et Magistra*.[82] These discussions were renewed again in light of the dissent over *Humanae Vitae*. Because these discussions indicate a possible disobedience of the authority of the hierarchy, some comment is needed to indicate the basis of this dissent.

Karl Rahner, a German Jesuit and a leading contemporary theologian, makes a general statement about obedience that sets the tone for his comments.

A subject in the Church can and should presume that the com-

---

[80] Carlo Cardinal Colombo, "Obedience to the Ordinary Magisterium." Quoted in Rahner, *op. cit.,* p. 64.

[81] *Lumen Gentium,* no. 37. Quoted in Abbott, *op. cit.,* p. 64.

[82] Charles Curran, "Catholic Ethics Today in the Light of the Dialogue with Protestant Ethics." Presidential Address to the American Society of Christian Ethics, 21 January 1972, p. 11 in the mimeographed text.

mand of an ecclesiastical superior does not violate the laws and norms of morality, but he cannot suppose *a priori* that, in every case, that is certain, and therefore he has the right and duty of judging in conscience about the morality of what is commanded.[83]

This statement strikes a good balance between respect for authority and the duties of conscience. It does not depreciate the values or rights of either, but neither does it give one total dominance over the other.

With reference to papal teaching, Rahner states that: "A papal pastoral letter which does not present any definition is basically a teaching that is capable of review."[84] This does not, however, dispense the Catholic from seriously considering the teaching. In this context, Rahner cites changes in papal teaching relative to democratic societies, pronouncements on biblical matters and some pronouncements on Modernism.[85] This leads Rahner to say that: "The authority of the magisterium in the Church and its respectability do not demand that a person act in the Church as if all theological positions are only the obedient repetition of a declaration of this magisterium."[86] Because of this there is an open system in the Church in which diverse factors—the insights of Christians and theologians and new situations proposing new questions—coalesce to clarify the faith and practice of the Church. This allows the possibility of reverent dissent or disobedience in good conscience to a non-infallible teaching of the hierarchy.

Bernard Haering also emphasizes the right to dissent based on the possibility of reform within non-infallible hierarchial teaching.[87] Haering gives examples of papal teachings that have been totally changed: the use of torture, usury, and religious freedom. Haering also argues for the possibility of disobedience on the basis of the weakness of the arguments used, especially

---

[83] Karl Rahner, S.J., "Christ as the Exemplar of Clerical Obedience." Quoted in Rahner, *op. cit.,* p. 5.

[84] Karl Rahner, S.J., "On the Encyclical *Humanae Vitae,*" *The National Catholic Reporter,* 18 September 1968, p. 6.

[85] *Ibid.,* p. 6.

[86] *Ibid.,* p. 7.

[87] Bernard Haering, C.SS.R., "The Encyclical Crisis," *Commonweal,* 6 September 1968, p. 588.

when these are based on natural law and form the right of freedom of speech within the Church which is necessary so that Christian growth can occur.[88] In response to the pope's reminder in the encyclical that obedience obliges because of both reasons given and more importantly because of the light given by the Holy Spirit to the teaching authority, Haering, referring to the history of the Church, replies that not everything that was said authoritatively within the Church can be ascribed automatically to the Holy Spirit. Haering also argues from the Scriptures that there is no necessity for all in the Church to speak with one language and one mentality.[89] Again, without denying authority or indicating an irresponsible disregard of the teachings of the hierarchy, Haering indicates the possibility of dissent within the Church.

What these two theologians point to is the possibility of what could be called a loyal opposition within the Church, not for the purpose of tearing down authority, but for the purpose of providing a corrective to it or to open authority to other points of view. The opinion of these men does not view obedience as a rubber-stamp nor does it see in obedience an easy way to avoid responsible decision-making. Authority and the demands of conscience are held in tension—but a tension that is creative and conducive to a greater development of the good of the whole Church. As Rahner says: "The sovereign worth of a sincere conscience is a greater good than the smooth running of the administration in any society, and especially, an ecclesiastical one."[90]

b. *Obedience to the State*

As has been noted in previous sections of this chapter, the traditional view of Roman Catholic social philosophy has been that the State indirectly reflects the authority of God and there-

[88] *Ibid.*, pp. 589-90.

[89] *Ibid.*, p. 592.

[90] Rahner, "Christ as the Exemplar of Clerical Obedience," *op. cit.*, pp. 5-6.

fore is worthy of obedience. Also as a product of the created order, the State has its own proper autonomy, structures and end. The citizen, as a part of this institution, has the duty to conform to the regulations which promote the common good. These are the religious and civil bases of the citizen's duty to obey civil authority. Also, as has been noted, emphasis has been placed on the presupposition of the justice of the State's commands, especially as this relates to what John Courtney Murray called the conscience of the law. The tradition gives witness to a primary obligation to obey the State.

Yet there is within this tradition an affirmation of a limited right to dissent from the authority of the State, but only when this contradicts the law of God. This is seen, within the tradition, as an exception, and a rare exception at that. But the tradition does indicate a tension between State and private conscience. A citizen cannot simply appeal to the rights of conscience as a way of avoiding political obligations; the State may not simply appeal to a citizen's duty to obey without seriously examining the questions of injustice raised by those engaging in dissent.[91] In this there is a parallel between dissent in the State and in the Church in that objective norms are appealed to and then tested for validity. This tension between obedience and dissent is also indicated by the Vatican Council's advice to make humane provision for conscientious objectors to war. The Council did not resolve the questions of which claims should take preference; it resolved the questions by calling for some exceptional provision.[92] Bernard Haering sums up the traditional position and indicates the tension it contains between obedience and authority by saying:

Only if authority itself recognizes the bond of conscience can the subject in conscience concede to it the presumption of right, of which we have just spoken. Law and command oblige only when they are in agreement with the norm of morals. It is not civil authority but conscience in conformity with the norm of

[91] Regan, "Conscience in the Documents of Vatican II," *op. cit.*, pp. 33-34.

[92] *Ibid.*, p. 36.

morals, which is the ultimate instance to which man appeals in rendering moral decisions.[93]

C. Summary Statement

With reference to the problem of obedience to the State, the Roman Catholic tradition has shown fidelity to several principles. The authority of the State is recognized as being an indirect reflection, in the created order, of the authority of God. Thus the State has a right to demand obedience of its citizens. Because the State operates on the basis of values, because there are moral standards built into its structure—John Courtney Murray's conscience of the laws—and because the State exists for the common good, a presumption of the justice of its demands and obligations must be given to it by the citizen. The weight of the Roman Catholic tradition is on the duty of the citizen to obey the State.

Yet this emphasis does not totally surrender the Roman Catholic citizen to the State. Although the Church is politically neutral, from a motive of Christian charity which is to be universal, and although the Church as such has no proper political, economic or social mission, the Church does demand that the laws of God and nature be observed, or at least not be contradicted by the State. The Church can serve, therefore, at times as an indirect judge on matters of State. This occurs when there is an obvious violation of the divine or natural law. Examples of this provided by tradition are genocide, damage to personal rights and harm to the common good. In instances of conflict in areas such as these, the Church demands fidelity to the law of God by its members.

In terms of the political obligations of the citizen, Roman Catholic tradition suggests a role that is largely passive. Emphasis is given to the citizen's duty to obey the State, not to any obligation to challenge the end the State is attempting to achieve or the strategies by which it will accomplish this. Voting is perceived as a serious duty, but the tradition leaves the

---

[93] Haering, *The Law of Christ,* Vol. 1, *op. cit.,* p. 150.

formation of the political conscience of the Catholic citizen in the hands of the State. This practice is validated by the natural law's recognition of the proper autonomy of the State and the presumption of the justice of its cause.

The tradition recognizes a limited right of dissent on the part of the Catholic citizen. This is an exceptional act, to be undertaken only when it is proved that the practice in question is contrary to either divine or natural law and when the dissent and its consequences will not cause greater injustice than already in the present situation. In practice, this right of dissent to civil authority has been developed mainly from a theoretical perspective; there has been little practice of this right and even fewer contributions to an analysis of the duty to dissent.

The Catholic citizen is in a position of being counseled to obey the State by both the Church and the State. The formation of conscience occurs in a context which emphasizes the prior right of authority. Individual decisions of conscience are discouraged because one individual cannot know all the facts to make a correct decision and because it is the role of authority to achieve the common good of all. Yet conscience and its rights are not denied. The tradition emphasizes that the conscience is the ultimate subjective norm of morality and that conscience, even though erroneous, must be followed. However, it is presumed that conscience will be in conformity with tradition and the interpretation of the tradition by the Church officials.

The general principles of the political obligations of the Roman Catholic citizen developed by the tradition are: (1) the duty to obey the State because it speaks indirectly with the authority of God; (2) a serious obligation to participate in electoral politics by voting; (3) the right to dissent from a command of the State if it is against the divine or natural law. This last obligation would seem to arise only when encouraged by the authority of the Church. Because of this perspective, the relation of the individual to the State is mainly passive. For although participation in politics, unions and other social agencies which will aid the development of society are encouraged, in the last analysis the fundamental obligation of the Catholic citizen is to obey the State with the quite certain knowledge that its policies are just and will achieve the common good. The active role of the Catholic citizen is predicated on the duty of obedience and the presumption of justice for the Catholic is to participate in the activities of the State to effect the achievement of its goals and values. Yet even this role is passive because it surrenders the choosing of goals and strategies to the State.

The weakness of the traditional Catholic concept of political obligation lies in its limited development of the duties of citizenship and in its emphasis on authority. Even though the Church as such has no proper political or social mission, it does possess values which have political and social implications. And these values should form the outline of a theory of ethical political obligation for the Roman Catholic citizen. These values must be utilized in examining the goals of society and the strategies adopted to achieve them. It is at this point that the Catholic citizen should be required to take a more active role. And it is at this point that the traditional analysis ends. This occurs because the individual is not encouraged to make this kind of analysis of society, because the individual does not have the knowledge that authority possesses, and because of the emphasis on obedience. Yet in a democratic society, this type of ethical activism should be encouraged because the citizen is responsible for the actions of his or her Government.

A case for a more active role for the Catholic citizen has been made by Zahn through his development of the concept of the Church's acting as a sect which emphasizes the prophetic dimension of the life of the Church. This concept stresses the role of the individual in the evaluation of the policies of both Church and State in relation to their proper mission. This sectarian dimension, which is not meant to place the Church in social isolation, is understood as a means of ensuring fidelity to primary values and as a corrective to perceived aberrations in the policies of either Church or State. This emphasis is supported by both Vatican II and contemporary theological evaluation. Following John XXIII's lead, Vatican II further developed the concept of the dignity of the human person and the rights of conscience. This analysis led to an evaluation which indicated a more active role for the individual within both Church and State. It also stressed the competence of the individual to make responsible moral evaluations, though this is not to be done in isolation from the ecclesiastical community. This means that while authority has a rightful and necessary place within the Church and its commands are to be heard and obeyed, this does not remove the possibility of the reformation or withdrawal of these teachings because they are not normally presented as infallible. Haering and Rahner both develop the point that conscience is influenced by more factors than the influence and the directives of the hierarchy of the Church. And it is from these other sources of morality, such as Scripture, the faith experience of the community, and the teaching of theologians, that corrective elements can arise. In this way the institutional Church, as well as public policy, actually can benefit from dissent through having important values pointed out and, as a consequence, giving the occasion and need to reexamine policies or teachings that may not in fact promote and serve the common good.

This chapter has provided a survey of the Roman Catholic tradition as it concerns the problem of the relation of the Catholic citizen to the State. The focal points of the tradition have been set forth from official documents and theological commentary. This summary has noted the specific points of emphasis within the tradition and has indicated some points of weakness within the traditional analysis. The task of the following chapters will be to provide a more thorough analysis of obedience to the State within the perspective of democratic societies. This will provide an occasion to give an analysis of the concept of obedience to the State and to suggest new points of departure, especially with reference to the concept of selective obedience to the State.

Chapter V
Selective Obedience and Democratic Government

The purpose of this chapter is to investigate the basis of political obligation within a democratic framework and to examine areas of Catholic theology which can provide possible points of departure for developing a theory of selective obedience to the State. The final section of this chapter will provide an analysis of the theory of selective obedience in relation to the concept of political obligation and thus set forth the ethical obligation of the Roman Catholic citizen in relation to the State.

A. Political Obligations in a Democratic Society

1. A General Description of Democrary in America

While democracy may be, as Churchill noted, the worst form of Government except for all the others that have been tried, it is the form of Government that has been the basis of American society for almost 200 years. In America, democracy is both representative and constitutional. This implies that the right to make political decisions is exercised by the people through elected representatives. Also the power of the majority is exercised within a constitution which guarantees the rights of the minority.[1] This system of Government allows the citizen

---

[1] "Democracy," *Encyclopaedia Britannica,* Vol. 7, 1969 ed., p. 215.

the opportunity to influence the substance of political decisions as well as the widest possible range of opinions to be taken into account in shaping these decisions.[2] Certain rights for the citizen also follow from this description of democracy: the right to vote, the right to represent others, and the right to freedom of speech.[3] These rights represent minimal structures for the participation of the citizen in the Government.

Two other areas, not specified by this description of democracy, which are important in the actualization of a democratic society are the concept of a citizen and the justness of the society. A brief discussion of these issues is important here because it will indicate other dimensions which must be taken into account in forming a concept of political obligation. These issues will not be resolved in this introductory section, but they are introduced here to indicate their significance.

Michael Walzer[4] presents several descriptions of citizens which indicate varying degrees of political involvement and obligation. Two common notions of citizenship are those of the citizen as a recipient of certain benefits which only the State can provide and the citizen as one who enjoys both liberty and protection by the authorities. However, the first category does not describe any political or moral dimensions of citizenship, while the second category says nothing about the activity of the citizen other than that of acknowledging the role of the State in protecting him or her.[5] This critique of traditional categories leads Walzer to provide a typology of different types of citizens. The first type is the oppressed citizen: "He counts for less than his fellows, sometimes for a great deal less, when it comes to the protection of life, liberty, property, and welfare."[6] The second is the alienated citizen: "He receives whatever protection the state provides. . . . But he does not participate at all in

---

[2] Harold J. Laski, *An Introduction to Politics* (London: George Allen and Unwen, Ltd., 1951), p. 57.

[3] Harold J. Laski, *A Grammar of Politics* (New Haven: Yale University Press, 1925), pp. 115-18.

[4] Michael Walzer, *Obligations: Essays on Disobedience, War and Citizenship* (Cambridge: Harvard University Press, 1970).

[5] *Ibid.,* pp. 205-206.

[6] *Ibid.,* p. 226.

political life. . . . He thinks of the state as an alien though not necessarily a hostile force, and he wants only to live in peace under its jurisdiction."[7] The final type is the pluralist citizen: "He receives protection and shares in ruling and being ruled, not in spite of his plural memberships, but because of them."[8] The concept of the pluralist citizen forms the basis for Walzer's definition of a citizen: one whose "largest or most inclusive group is the state."[9] This implies that the citizen is not simply a citizen of the State, but is one who also has responsibilities to the other associations of which he or she is a member. The strength that Walzer sees in the pluralist definition of citizenship is that, "it not only implicates the citizen in state policy, but generates real obligations and an authentic patriotism by recognizing a sphere within which they actually have scope for meaningful action."[10]

The typology and definition raise questions about the types of obligation incurred by each type of citizen and in particular the possibility of conflict of obligation on the part of the pluralist citizen. This possibility of conflict is also raised by the problem of justice within a democratic society. Justice here can be viewed from two perspectives: the ends chosen to be attained by the society and the procedures adopted to achieve goals, which may, as yet, be unspecified. Rawls and Childress place emphasis on justice being located within the procedures of the Government.[11] This emphasizes the conditions under which justice may be a reality within a society as well as affirming a doctrine of obligation based on implicit consent to these conditions and procedures. A limitation of this emphasis on procedural justice is the fact that the outcome of the procedure itself may not be just. The point is that a just structure is not necessarily a guarantee of just social decisions.

The issue of social justice, which in general refers to the

---

[7] *Loc. cit.*

[8] *Ibid.*, p. 227.

[9] *Ibid.*, p. 218.

[10] *Ibid.*, p. 220.

[11] John Rawls, *A Theory of Justice* (Cambridge: The Belknap Press, 1971), p. 7. Also see James Childress, *Civil Disobedience and Political Obligation* (New Haven: Yale University Press, 1971), p. 156.

distribution of rights and duties and equality of opportunity,[12] is also related to the problem of political obligation. Those who are effectively cut out of the political system and who are victims of injustice may find themselves in the position of being alienated citizens with a minimal perception of obligation to the Government. The issue raised is the degree of obligation on the part of the citizen when either the procedures or the programs of the Government are unjust. The criteria for this need further explication, which will be presented later in the chapter.

What this introduction suggests is that the problem of political obligation is related in a crucial way to the effective participation of the citizen in the life of the State and to the justice of the State, both in its procedures and its programs. These are two significant issues related in particular to the problem of political obligation in American democracy.

2. Sources of Political Obligation

In a democratic society, obligation is typically described as arising out of membership in the society, consent to the policies of the society and the principle of justice or fairness. Each of these will be examined to arrive at a description of political obligation. It should also be noted that the authority of the State as a source of obligation is a presupposition of this section. The problem of this section is to ascertain what obligation the citizens have in relation to this authority, or what circumstances will qualify their obligations to the State.

a. *Membership in the Society*

Residence in a democratic society creates a *prima facie* obligation for obedience to the State, according to Walzer, for three reasons: (1) because of the benefits that are received;

---

[12] Consult Rawls, *op. cit.*, p. 7.

(2) because of the expectations aroused among one's fellow citizens; (3) because of the universality of obligation within a democratic society.[13] Residence, however, creates minimal membership which is the point of departure for a concept of political obligation. Significant obligations come only with willful membership, a conscious acceptance of the State and commitment to it by actions.[14] The *prima facie* obligation is qualified, then, by the degree of the willfulness of the membership. Walzer argues that neither living in a State nor accepting its benefits can constitute the source of ultimate obligation to the State. This situation occurs mainly because the society into which we are born is rarely the State in which we choose membership.[15] Also one dimension of citizenship is to be "committed to a political system, not merely to the survival of the society that system organizes, but to the survival of the particular organization and also to all those purposes beyond survival that the organization needs for itself."[16] Such commitment cannot come from mere residence but only from willful commitment.

The depth of commitment to a society can also be discerned through examination of the citizen's membership in secondary associations which have limited claims to primacy. Membership in these types of associations may constitute alternatives to membership in the State or at least weaken its claims. This situation creates a type of "internal emigration"[17] from the State and is an attempt to seek other goods. Membership in such a group may limit the obligation of the citizen to the State for while it is true that the State does seek to provide its members with goods, it is not always the case that these goods add up to the common good or the highest good. If the good sought by the secondary associations is a good higher than the good proposed by the State, the obligation to the State is weakened considerably.[18]

This means that most citizens are pluralists, in the sense

13 Walzer, *op. cit.,* p. 28
14 *Ibid.,* p. 7.
15 *Ibid.,* p. 112.
16 *Ibid.,* p. 105.
17 *Ibid.,* p. 18.
18 *Ibid.,* pp. 19-20.

described above. Whether they choose other groups because of personal alienation or lack of power within the system or because of identification with the goals of other associations, it is possible to qualify membership in the State by such associations. The obligation of the pluralist citizen is divided among his or her different groups, each of which makes claims upon him or her which affect the claims of other groups. Thus, although political obligations do arise from the simple fact of residence, these obligations may be qualified through an internal emigration to secondary associations which seek other goods and which make valid claims upon the allegiance of the citizen, as well as actual willfulness of membership.

b. *Consent*

In all consent or contract theories, obligation arises from the agreement of the citizen to accept the Government. This may be done in an explicit fashion, through deliberate participation in the political processes, or may be done tacitly, through the acceptance of the benefits of the State. In this way, obligation arises as the result of a voluntary act and its content is defined by the institution to which the citizen consents.[19] Also implied in this consent is an acceptance of the defects of an institution and restraint in taking advantage of them, for without this restraint, moral trust and confidence will break down.[20]

But while acceptance of the benefits of the Government may imply tacit consent and therefore acceptance of obligations, the problem arises as to the degree to which tacit consent binds. For the obligations incurred by silence, obedience to law and the keeping of the public peace are the same as those owed to society at large and would not seem to be the basis of any ultimate obligation to the State.[21] Also, as Laski noted, if we make consent the source of the obligation of obedience to the State, the citizen maintains the duty to examine continually

---

[19] Rawls, *op. cit.*, p. 113.
[20] *Ibid.*, p. 355.
[21] Walzer, *op. cit.*, pp. 100-101.

the policies of the State.[22] This is also affirmed by Walzer who suggests that consent is not necessarily given at once but that it comes, rather, by degrees and is therefore open to continual evaluation.[23] And obligations arising out of consent are further qualified by Arendt who says that promises are qualified by two limitations: (1) no unexpected situations can arise; (2) the mutuality inherent in the promise must not be broken.[24]

Another source of obligation, then, is consent which is a reciprocal commitment to the State on the part of the citizen. But this consent is neither blind nor irrevocable. For although consent, or even tacit consent, is binding and constitutes a source of obligation, it can be given gradually and the act of consenting implies a continual examination of the policies of the institutions to which we commit ourselves.

c. *Justice*

The role of justice is important in determining obligation because we can be obligated only to that which has a moral claim upon us. In Walzer's words: "When justice is not done, there is no legitimate state and no obligation to obey."[25] The problem comes when one is called upon to describe justice and provide criteria by which one can judge the justice of an institution. Some contemporary efforts have been made in this direction and can provide a point of reference for a discussion of justice.

Mulford Sibley uses both procedural norms and substantive priorities as his criteria of the justice or legitimacy of a Government.[26] A Government which refuses to hear criticisms,

---

[22] Harold J. Laski, *Authority in the Modern State* (New Haven: Yale University Press, 1927), pp. 46-47.

[23] Walzer, *op. cit.,* p. xiii.

[24] Hannah Arendt, *Crises of the Republic* (New York: Harcourt Brace Jovanovich, Inc., 1972), p. 93.

[25] Walzer, *op. cit.,* p. 50.

[26] Mulford Sibley, "On Political Obligation and Civil Disobedience," *Journal* of the Minnesota Academy of Science, Vol. 33, No. 1 (1965), pp. 70-71.

which reduces freedom of expression or which withholds information is unjust in its procedures. Also, if its priorities are inadequate, the same criticism can be made. Sibley recognizes the possibility of the relative injustice of the State arising from a mixture of just and unjust claims. And even though the order is only partially just, the value of order, "is so great that unless the system can be shown to be gravely deficient in its moral underpinnings, it must be assumed to have a certain claim, however bastardized."[27] In this case, obligation exists in relation to the legitimate authority which approximates the greatest degree of justice. This differs from Walzer who bases obligation on willfulness of membership and competing claims from secondary associations.

In a recently published work, James Childress argues that the basis for moral obligation in a democratic society can be accounted for most adequately in terms of political relations between citizens, in particular by a specification of the concept of fair play.[28] In this perspective, political obligation arises out of the relationship between citizens, not between citizens and the authorities as Sibley argues. This obligation is incurred by the acceptance of the benefits of an ordered body politic, "which would not have been possible without the general obedience and cooperation of one's fellow citizens."[29] In this situation, when it comes my turn to obey the law, I am obligated to do so because in doing this I act fairly in relation to those whose obedience made possible both the structure and its benefits. This situation constitutes a moral claim on me by my fellow citizens.[30] Obligation in this sense arises from the behavior of other citizens who have restricted their behavior and freedom in the expectation that I and other citizens would act in a similar fashion.[31] Childress does not argue that the duty of fair play constitutes an ultimate source of obligations—because other *prima facie* obligations may conflict with it—but he does

---

[27] *Ibid.*, p. 71.

[28] Childress, *op. cit.*, p. 120.

[29] *Ibid.*, p. 131.

[30] *Ibid.*, p. 138.

[31] *Ibid.*, p. 135.

emphasize that political obligation is an act of justice and therefore places a moral obligation on the citizen to obey.[32]

John Rawls, in a thorough analysis of the concept of justice from a contemporary contractarian viewpoint, describes some dimensions of political obligations. Two bases of obligation enunciated by Rawls of importance for a theory of political obligation are the principles of fairness and the natural duty of justice. The principle of fairness states that a person is required to do his part as defined by the rules of an institution when two conditions are met: (1) the institution is just or fair; (2) one has accepted or taken advantage of the benefits offered by the institution.[33] The natural duty of justice requires us to support and comply with just institutions that exist and apply to us.[34] Rawls argues here that if an institution is just, there is a natural duty to obey. "Each is bound to those institutions independent of his voluntary acts, performance or otherwise. Thus even though the principles of natural duty are derived from a contractarian point of view, they do not presuppose an act of consent, express or tacit, or indeed any voluntary act, in order to apply."[35]

The two principles of justice that Rawls proposes as a test to determine whether institutions have a claim on our obedience are:

1. Each person is to have an equal right to the most extensive liberty compatible with a similar liberty for others.

2. Social and economic inequalities are to be arranged so that they are (a) reasonably expected to be to everyone's advantage, and (b) attached to positions and offices open to all.[36]

Within this context, Rawls argues that when people engage in mutually advantageous enterprises according to rules and restrict their liberty so that all may gain advantage, "those who

[32] *Ibid.*, p. 164.
[33] Rawls, *op. cit.*, p. 112.
[34] *Ibid.*, p. 115.
[35] *Ibid.*, p. 115.
[36] *Ibid.*, p. 60.

have submitted to these restrictions have a right to a similar acquiescence on the part of those who have benefited from their submission. We are not to gain from the cooperative labors of others without doing our share."[37]

Rawls bases obligation on two sources: the natural obedience owed in justice to an institution that is just and the reciprocal duties among citizens who restrict their behavior for one another's mutual advantage.

3. Summary Statement

From this analysis, there are two sources of political obligation that present strong *prima facie* obligations: the natural authority of the State which is constituted by the acceptance of its constitution and the relation between the citizens who restrict their liberty and behavior for their mutual advantage in the expectation that others will act in a similar way.

The major presupposition for the obligation of obedience arising out of this description is the justice, or relative justice, of the State. In its minimal form the test of justice consists in the distribution of rights and duties within society and the equality of opportunity for all. This concept would be testable through the use of both procedural and substantive norms such as suggested by Rawls and Sibley. Even the fact of relative injustice does not destroy the strength of this *prima facie* obligation to obey for as Rawls notes: "We are to recognize unjust laws as binding provided that they do not exceed certain limits of injustice."[38] This excess comes from a departure from publicly accepted standards of justice and from arrangements conforming only to the needs of a special interest group.[39] Childress argues that the obligation to obey unjust laws stems from the fact that in so doing, "one shares the burdens, risks, and restrictions of cooperation in a project of fallible men whose sense of justice is not sharply honed and is frequently dulled

---

[37] *Ibid.*, p. 112.
[38] *Ibid.*, p. 351.
[39] *Ibid.*, p. 352.

by their propensity toward injustice."[40] Fair play here demands that inconvenience, as well as advantages, be equally shared. The obligation of the citizen to obey can be weakened or negated, therefore, only through appeal to commonly shared concepts of justice and the public conception of justice by which citizens regulate their affairs and interpret their constitution.[41]

The theories of obligation presented by Rawls and Childress indicate solid arguments for the duty of obedience to the State. What they do not take into account, however, is Walzer's notion of pluralistic citizenship. In addition to being obligated by the natural authority of the State (Rawls) and my relations with my fellow citizens (Childress), I am also obligated by the other associations of which I am a member. In addition to my relation to the State and other citizens, I am related to secondary associations which I have voluntarily joined and which constitute other sources of obligations which may qualify these other *prima facie* obligations to State and citizens. The concept of pluralistic citizenship does not negate the theories of Rawls and Childress but indicates other sources of obligation which the citizen must evaluate in defining the degree of obligation owed to the State in a particular instance. The political obligations of the citizen come from three basic sources: the obligation to obey just institutions that exist and apply to us (Rawls); the responsibility owed by one citizen to his or her fellow citizens as specified by the concept of fair play (Childress); and the claims of secondary associations of which the citizen is a member as specified by the concept of the pluralist citizen (Walzer). Sibley's notions of procedural and substantive criteria for determining obligation should be related to Rawls' discussion of the qualifications of obedience.

The theories of Walzer, Rawls, Childress and Sibley are not necessarily mutually contradictory. They rather indicate sources of obligation that arise from different relationships. In this they are mutually corrective and indicate areas of tension in the citizen's articulating the degree of obligation owed the State

---

[40] Childress, *op. cit.*, p. 158.
[41] Rawls, *op. cit.*, p. 365.

by indicating the various claims of institutions and groups upon the citizen.

These contractual theories of obligation present an initial challenge to the traditional Roman Catholic doctrine of obligation which is grounded in the individual's participation in an hierarchically structured society and his or her place in the order of the universe. The traditional Roman Catholic teaching does not emphasize the competence of the individual to choose his or her obligations, as previous chapters have demonstrated. However, recent encyclicals and the documents of Vatican II have indicated that civil authority must be in conformity with divine authority and that there are times when the citizen may legitimately dissent, the three major instances being genocide, damage to personal rights and significant harm to the common good. It is in this area that there is an opening to relate elements of contractual theory to Roman Catholic natural law philosophy to develop a theory of selective obedience to the State. The remaining sections of this chapter indicate how this is to be accomplished.

B. The Problem of Selective Obedience

The previous section sketched out some elements of political obligation in terms of its origins and limitations. This section is concerned with setting forth some theological positions that have a bearing on the problem of selective obedience to the State. The analysis done in this section does not have as its purpose the setting forth of ethical obligations (this will be done in the following section); its purpose is to illuminate certain theological dimensions of the Church that point to the relation of the Church and its members to the State. This will be done to clarify the principles which will provide the ethical basis of the political obligation of the Roman Catholic citizen.

1. The Problem of the Church in Society

The relation of the Church to society has been the subject

of many analyses, from the church-sect typologies of Troeltsch to the Christ-culture categories of H. Richard Niebuhr, as well as studies on denominationalism as a middle ground between the church-sect types, especially in the American religious experience. These studies have concentrated on the issues of compromise, prophecy and the opposition of some values of the larger society on the part of the Church as well as giving attention to the problem of individual needs versus responsibility to the larger society. Though these studies have not resolved the issues raised, they have indicated various problems that must be kept in mind as one analyzes the role of the Church in a specific area.

The Roman Catholic Church has one of the better claims to the church type in the light of its history, structure, and its relation to the societies with which it finds itself in association. In terms of its articulation of a theory of Church-State relations and the actual practice of these relations that have been discussed in previous chapters, it is evident that the Church is anxious to maintain positive relations with the State and will, on occasion, go to great lengths to accommodate itself to the State. The problem raised by the history of the Church is not that the Church has proved to be a disruptive institution, but rather that the Church finds it easy to accept the policies of the State. Also in terms of the tradition of the Church, the emphasis of the teaching magisterium and the teaching of individual theologians the Church has, for all practical purposes, taught that total obedience must be given to the State. The sole exception, which has possibly expired because of over-qualification, has been the reminder that we must obey God rather than men.

The tradition and the practice of the Church suggest a policy of selective dissent to the State because the tradition is based on the obligation of the citizen to obey the State. This book proposes instead that the stance of the Church and its members should be one of selective or qualified obedience to the State based on the need continually to examine the moral implications of the policies of the State to determine whether obedience should be given or withheld in a particular case.

The first argument for this position will be in terms of the relation of the Church to society.

That the Roman Catholic Church fits the church typology cannot be denied. Nor can the history of the Church's acting in this fashion be ignored. Yet, because of the dissolution of the medieval culture in which the church type was realized most perfectly and because of the position of the Church in contemporary society, it is not evident that the Church will always be able to perform in the mode of the church type. Particularly in America is this the case. For here all religious institutions basically perform as a denomination or a sect relative to the larger society, which implies that their relations to society in a particular instance are not clearly defined or predictable. Neither can we always assume a coincidence of values or strategies on the part of the Church and State. Religious institutions may have a set of values that demand specific behavior that is contrary to the life of the larger society. In this instance the Church may be called upon to act as a sect, that is, to stand in opposition to the larger society in defense of values crucial to its own self-understanding and hierarchy of values.[42]

This position, which can also be described as prophetic, assumes a relation between Church and State that is not determined *a priori*. It demands a constant evaluation of the policies and strategies of the State in relation to the values and religious objectives of the Church, as well as public policy. Also the position of the Church may not necessarily be able to be translated totally into a political strategy or an argument based completely on public policy. Rather, the Church, in this instance, acts out of a position of defending a religious value, the practice of which is perceived as crucial to the life of the Church. This action of the Church is to give authentic religious witness to its own life and traditions and therefore it occasionally can and must take a stand against the policies of the larger society or the authority of the State.

The life and tradition of the religious institution, together

---

[42] This point is suggested and developed by Gordon Zahn, *In Solitary Witness, op. cit.*, p. 203.

with the commitment of the individual to the institution, constitutes a set of obligations for its members. The Church, acting
as a form of social control, claims the right to demand conformity to these values so that it may be faithful to its own
nature and value structure. This may occasion the necessity of
its acting in the manner of a sect with respect to the defense of
values crucial to its nature and existence. In this instance the
Church provides membership in a secondary, voluntary association which qualifies the obligations owed to other groups. This
Church membership constitutes the Catholic as a pluralist citizen in Walzer's terminology and his or her obligations to the
State must be examined and possibly qualified in the light of
the values of the Catholic Church.

2. The Problem of Values

Both Church and State support value systems, orientate the
lives of their members around them, and serve as agents of
social control to achieve the attainment of their goals.

The Roman Catholic Church, both through its acceptance
of the New Testament and the development of the doctrine of
natural law, has developed a specific set of transcendent norms
that are to be used as points of reference in judging specific
actions of its members. The content of these values may be
related to the discussion of the development of cross-cultural
or thematic values. Even though some of the values of the
Church, such as faith and hope, may be specifically religious
values, the social values, such as justice, respect for the truth,
and respect for human dignity, promulgated by the Church's
social philosophy, are positively related to many of the values
of the larger society and the value structures of other nations.

The problem that arises here is that at times the Church
will insist on a particular definition of a value or a specific
mode of action to fulfill the value that will not necessarily be
in accord with the definition of this value by the larger society.
The Church, on the basis of revelation and natural law, maintains—in theory, at least—an absolute point of reference in its
definition of values. This can create a situation in which the

Church may insist upon more thematic values than the State is willing to admit, as well as ways of implementing them which may not be approved by a majority of the citizens of the State.

The issue here is not the method of arriving at values or of defining their content. Society does recognize the existence of thematic or cross-cultural values. And the Roman Catholic Church, because of its value-commitments, has a positive contribution to make to this continuing debate over the definition of values. The Church has religious values proper to its own life[43] and values that are of importance to all of human society. By its adherence to these values, the Church can offer criticism of the values of the State and can help in the defining of thematic values.[44] This type of confrontation of values will be ensured if the Church has demanded that its members accept certain values or norms as absolute for this will place one group of citizens in conflict with other groups. The Catholic will be in the position of qualifying his or her relation to certain social values on the basis of religious conviction. In this way, through the Roman Catholic Church's insistence on certain transcendent values, it imposes on both the institution and the individual member a position of selective behavior in a society which does not accept all of these values and norms. It is also brought into dialogue with the larger society over the meaning of these values and this contributes to the common good. Through this process, selective obedience contributes a positive dimension to an articulation of cross-cultural values.

3. The Problem of the Common Good

Pope John XXIII defined the common good as the "sum of

---

[43] Though these values may be specifically religious, such as faith, hope and charity, it may not be assumed that they contribute nothing to political life or a critique of the society. The development of political theology, for example, is partially rooted in a development of the virtue of hope.

[44] This is not meant in a triumphalistic sense or that all values must conform to the definition accepted by Roman Catholicism. The point is, simply, that through maintaining a particular point of view, the Church can offer an alternative point of view.

those conditions of social living, whereby men are enabled more fully and more readily to achieve their own perfection."[45] This definition was used by Vatican II and also forms the basis of Paul VI's discussion of the conditions of human life demanded by the common good. Negatively, Paul VI teaches that the lack of material necessities and oppressive social structures, abuses of political and economic power, and unjust transactions must be removed so that the common good may be obtained. Positively, he teaches that the acquisition of knowledge and culture, victory over disease, respect for human dignity, co-operation for peace, the acknowledgement of supreme values and union with God form the contemporary dimensions of the common good.[46]

The problem with the concept of the common good is that it may either be a conservative or a progressive principle. In the examination of the traditions of the Church, reference was made to the fact that unjust authority should be obeyed within the limits of the common good. There was also present an emphasis on the value of order which implies that social structures should not be disturbed or violated because they approximated the realization of the common good. The doctrine of the common good has also been used to affirm the political obligation of a rather total obedience to the authority of the State.[47] Seen from this perspective, the common good functions as a legitimating principle of the contemporary condition of society. Because elements in society are seen as reflections of various dimensions of the common good, dissent is viewed as an act which, on the one hand, endangers the goods actually attained and, on the other hand, can interfere with the actualization of other goods made possible by the relative justice of the structure itself. In this way, the concept of the common good serves as a conservative norm, inhibiting dissent and disobedience.

---

[45] John XXIII, *Mater et Magistra,* quoted in Gibbons, *Seven Great Encyclicals, op. cit.,* p. 233.

[46] Paul VI, *Progressio Populorum* (Boston: Daughters of St. Paul, 1967), pp. 13-14.

[47] *Gaudium et Spes,* quoted in Abbott, *The Documents of* Vatican II, *op. cit.,* p. 284.

Yet it is possible to view the common good as a means of grounding a doctrine of selective obedience to the State. The opening for this comes from the relative justice of the social structure within which the concept of the common good is operative. Relative justice, of course, implies relative injustice. Thus, as Pope Paul affirmed, oppressive social structures, economic injustice and the arbitrary use of political authority constitute failures to achieve the common good. Another characteristic of the common good is that "all members be entitled to share in it, although in different ways according to each one's tasks, merits and circumstance."[48] This means that the common good, though attained in different ways by individuals, cannot be for the advantage of only a select few. If it is the case that the benefits of the common good, especially in terms of employment, political equality and social justice, are not being extended to all the citizens—especially to those in need or to those who are powerless—the Catholics who are citizens could claim a right to limit their support of the Government, especially in those areas where the injustice is manifest. A Government of limited justice may deserve only limited support because its benefits are not equally extended. This does not argue that the Catholic citizen is relieved of all obligations to the Government; it is arguing that because of the relative injustice present within the Government and society, the Roman Catholic citizen has the right and duty to qualify his or her support of and obedience to the State.

4. The Problem of Membership in Church and State

The Roman Catholic is a member of two institutions which have different purposes and ends, but which should generally be compatible in terms of objectives to be achieved. A description of these institutions from the perspective of their value commitments will help illuminate the problem of selective obedience to the State.

---

[48] John XXIII, *Pacem in Terris,* quoted in *Seven Great Encyclicals, op. cit.,* p. 301.

The State is a primary institution by virtue of the inclusiveness of its membership and its concern for all of its members. The Government of the State can be representative of many differing opinions and a variety of interest groups. Yet, though the State is a primary association, it does not follow that its values or goals are primary values. One of the main values of the State is its own existence. Another is the order in society which allows the structures of the State to function smoothly. In short, though the State may profess and pledge itself to values such as justice, freedom and equality, the State does not tend to be a self-critical institution. Because of this, the State may operate at the level of ideology[49] rather than the level of value and self-criticism. The citizen finds himself or herself in a position of being a member of a State which may have the widest possible appeal in terms of membership but may have a very narrow appeal in terms of value commitment. The State may be described as a primary institution with secondary values.

In describing the Church from this perspective, it is evident that it is a secondary association because of the limitation of membership—in terms of the requirement of a faith commitment—and the selectivity of its values. Regardless of its history, the main value and goal of the Church is the transcendent—union with God in the establishment of the Kingdom. Because of this, the Church's primary values are religious and its main concern is the sanctification of its members. This implies that, from a certain perspective, the Church can be an institution that is more likely to be self-critical, for its own existence is not a primary value. The constant tradition has been that the Church will give way to the Kingdom and therefore the Church is a temporary reality constantly attempting to surpass itself in achieving the total realization of its end. The Church's primary goal is the Kingdom which is a future event; this allows the Church to be self-critical because it realizes that no one stage of its history is definitive or the full realization of its

---

[49] Ideology is being used in Mannheim's sense of thinking that is so interest bound to a situation that no other factors can be seen. Consult Karl Mannheim, *Ideology and Utopia* (New York: Harcourt, Brace, and World, Inc., 1935), p. 40.

values. The Church therefore can be described as a secondary association with primary values.

The potential conflict of values between Church and State is more clearly revealed by this description of membership and value commitment. The possibility of selectivity in obedience to the State arises because of the conflict between primary and secondary values in institutions that are socially interrelated. The values of the Church supersede the values of the State because of their transcendence and possible freedom from ideology. The Roman Catholic who is a citizen must always, therefore, order his or her political obligations in the light of his or her transcendent values because they have an ultimate claim upon him or her.[50]

This section has presented four general arguments for selective obedience to the State: the necessity of the Church occasionally acting as a sect, the problem of conflicting or competing values between Church and State, the demands of the common good, and fidelity to the primary values proclaimed by the secondary association of the Church. The purpose of these arguments is to propose an alternative point of view in describing the Catholic citizen's obligations to the State. The following section will specify this further by discussing the ethical dimensions of selective obedience.

C. The Ethical Obligations of a Roman Catholic Citizen

In discussing Catholic principles of politics, John Ryan provides a summary statement of the traditional understanding of the duties of the Catholic citizen. He describes the first duty as that of obedience to the law. This may be a grave obligation

---

[50] The point being made here should not be understood in such a way that it would be limited only to Roman Catholicism. The superiority of a Church's values over those of the State is a universal principle of Christianity, and possible of all groups with a transcendent claim. This principle is being examined here with special reference to Catholicism; it will be discussed in reference to other groups in the concluding chapter of the book.

if the subject matter of the law is serious and the legislator intends the law to bind in conscience in this fashion.[51] A second duty is respect for public officials and their enactments. Related to this is the duty of loyalty, i.e., faithfulness and constancy in allegiance and service. Other duties, described as elementary, are the paying of taxes and participation in military service.[52] The duty of paying taxes is based on the obligation of the citizen to help meet the requirements of the common good. The duty of military service is described as "an obligation gravely binding in conscience."[53] A second class of duties arises as a result of electoral functions. These consist in the duty to vote, to vote in a manner conducive to the common good, to base one's vote on principles, and to acquire the knowledge to cast a responsible vote.[54]

These obligations are based on legal justice, "the virtue that inclines the citizen to render to the community what is due it for the common good."[55] As such, this description of the political obligations of the Catholic citizen focuses on minimal obligations and has as its presupposition the justice of the State and the implication that obedience is to be given to the State as a matter of course.[56] The problem with a position such as this is that it can legitimate an uncritical participation in civil life and can implicitly assume a separation between civil life and religious life, a type of dualism condemned by Vatican II.[57] The duties described by Ryan are mainly passive and do not seriously describe the relation of the citizen to the State in the

---

[51] John A. Ryan and Francis J. Boland, *Catholic Principles of Politics* (New York: The Macmillan Company, 1940), p. 184.

[52] *Ibid.*, p. 201.

[53] *Ibid.*, p. 203.

[54] *Ibid.*, pp. 205-206.

[55] *Ibid.*, p. 194.

[56] Ryan says that loyalty implies an habitual spirit and attitude toward the laws: a presupposition exists in favor of organic and statutory enactments and principles. The loyal citizen is to give the Government the benefit of the doubt and to withhold obedience only when doubt is converted into moral certainty. Ryan summarizes this by saying that the habitual attitude of the loyal citizen is sympathetic faith, not distrust. *Ibid.*, p. 198.

[57] *Gaudium et Spes,* quoted in Abbott, *The Documents of Vatican II, op. cit.*, p. 243.

light of Church membership. Important as the duties that Ryan describes are, they do not seem to hit at the heart of a Christian's obligations to the State because they presume a congruence of values between Church and State and because they do not provide a critical examination of the Catholic's responsibility to God or to the Church. The following framework is offered as a way of providing ethical norms which can give the basis for a responsible analysis of the political obligations of the Catholic citizen.

Membership in the Roman Catholic Church implies a certain set of religious obligations which have significant political applications and consequences. The first of these is the totality of the individual's commitment to God. This is a declaration that God is the highest value in the individual's life and ultimate union with God the goal of all the individual's actions. Also, for Catholics, this relation to God is mediated through the Church. This implies fidelity to religious creeds and the codes of morality of the Church because these are means of the individual's entering union with God and a way of concretizing fidelity to God. Obedience to the Church is not to be equated with obedience to God, but obedience to the Church is one important way of expressing this type of relationship within Roman Catholicism. This is because the Church, as described by Vatican II, is a "kind of sacrament or sign of intimate union with God, and of the unity of all mankind. She is also an instrument for the achievement of such union and unity."[58] This means that the person's ultimate loyalty to God is actualized through membership and participation in the Church. In this way, the claims of the Church on the individual are seen as religious obligations which inhere in the individual's relation with God. The teaching magisterium of the Church has the right to define certain values as being critical relative to one's relation with God.

Another dimension of the Church, which was given a new emphasis by Vatican II, is that the Church is the Kingdom of

---

[58] *Lumen Gentium,* quoted in Abbott, *The Documents of Vatican II, op. cit.*, p. 15.

God now present in mystery.[59] This means that the Church is a temporary phenomenon and will receive its fulfillment only in the establishment of the Kingdom of God. No institutional form of the Church is definitive, although the Church must exist as an institution. No mode of self-expression or theology may be seen as definitive, although the Church must define itself and express its life in ritual and creed. When the Church is faithful to its eschatological nature, it realizes that its fulfillment comes only from the future—the Kingdom—and that the life it lives now and the faith it expresses are an incomplete articulation of the mystery of the Kingdom that it now bears in an earthen vessel. The Church must be its own critic for while it knows the presence of God in Christ and the significance of its religious values, the Church also knows full well that it only partially incarnates these realities in its life and that there is a continual need for a greater degree of actualization of these values.[60]

The members of the Church express belief in and commitment to God through membership in the Church. By this the members enter into a mediated, sacramental relationship with God. This entails the acceptance and living out of values which, while normative, stand in continual need of actualization in the members' lives because of the very eschatological nature of the Church. The need for renewal in the teaching of the Church has been discussed previously in the section on conscience and obedience to the teaching magisterium of the Church. The theological basis for the possibility of dissent in the Church and society relative to the mode of the implementation of values comes from the eschatological nature of the Church. Within this framework, ecclesiastical authority and obedience are seen as necessary and related theologically to the rule of Christ within the Church, but the obligations ensuing from this are not seen as being able to be univocally once for all. Membership in this eschatological community brings obligations, but the implementation of these stands always under the judgment of the Kingdom. For the members of the Church,

---

59 *Ibid.,* p. 16.
60 *Ibid.,* p. 24.

the Kingdom of God is the highest value and all else in the Church must be judged in its light.

Even though the Church is an eschatological community and receives its fulfillment in the future establishment of the Kingdom of God, it exists now as an institution which inter-penetrates and interacts with other institutions. It is therefore proper for the Church to act, at this stage of its history, as an institution. Even though the Church as such has no primary political or social mission,[61] its members are citizens of nation-states; in this sense, the Church can be said to have a social mission arising from this indirect relation to social issues. This situation of living in at least two major institutions raises the question of how to determine the political obligations of the Roman Catholic citizen.

Because of this commitment to God, expressed through membership in the Church, the Roman Catholic citizen qualifies for the category of the pluralist citizen described by Walzer which specifies that citizens share in ruling and being ruled because of plural memberships.[62] There are two reasons for this: (1) as a Catholic, the citizen belongs to a group that may make claims against the State; (2) as a Catholic and a citizen, the individual has obligations from these two associations and must decide between competing values and the obligations they imply. This may be done through the use of the procedural and substantive criteria developed by Sibley for determining the justice of the State's policy and its consequent obligatory nature. As a citizen of the nation-state, the Catholic must take seriously the authority of his or her Government and his or her own obligations to the State for he or she has accepted benefits from the State and has, to some extent, shared in the political processes, at least by voting. These *prima facie* obligations must be evaluated, however, by the Catholic in the light of the value system of the Church. This implies a procedural as well as a substantive analysis of the goals and strategies of

---

[61] *Gaudium et Spes,* quoted in Abbott, *The Documents of Vatican II, op. cit.,* p. 241.

[62] Walzer, *Obligations, op. cit.,* p. 227. This is discussed in Section A of this chapter.

the nation-state. The *prima facie* obligations are then affirmed or qualified through this ethical evaluation.

Pluralism, in the sense of membership in primary and secondary associations, does not relieve the citizen of political obligations incurred through the acceptance of benefits from and protection by the Government, participation in the electoral process, or a principle of fairness which implies mutual restrictions on behavior. What pluralist citizenship does imply is that the political obligations of a citizen are qualified by the claims and values of the secondary associations to which the citizen belongs. From the perspective of this model of pluralist citizenship and the ultimacy of the claim of God on the individual expressed through membership in the Church, the proper relation of the Roman Catholic citizen to the State would seem to be one of selective obedience. This is a proper description because it is a theory of obedience to the State; yet, the obedience due the State is, because of religious commitments claiming priority and ultimacy, an obedience that can be qualified or selective in its nature. A theory of selective obedience requires that competing claims be evaluated in the light of more inclusive value commitments, especially religious ones, and that primacy be given to those which are more ultimate. In this way, political obligations become qualified and obedience necessarily becomes more selective.

As described by John Courtney Murray, who based his analysis on both tradition and the formulations of Vatican II, the State is an autonomous reality with its own laws, conscience and values. The State has its own process of decision-making; it can make claims upon individuals because of their membership and because of the justice of its cause. Its claims to moral authority come primarily from the following of established political procedures,[63] as well as from the justice of its cause. Moral claims also arise, following Childress' analysis, from the spirit of fair play among citizens and, in the opinion of Rawls, the natural duty of justice which obliges us to comply with just institutions that exist and apply to us. But these moral

---

[63] Consult John Courtney Murray, "War and Conscience," *op. cit.,* pp. 26ff.

claims constitute only a *prima facie* obligation to obey the State. They are, in fact, only one set of obligations among others that have a claim on the citizen who is a member of other associations. As such, the obligation of obedience to the State must be analyzed in the light of other obligations; its moral claim on the citizen is relative to its ability to go beyond a *prima facie* obligation and to establish its value against the competing claims of other obligations.

In terms of this competition of claims, the tradition of the Roman Catholic Church has always insisted on the absoluteness of God's claim on the person. This is traditionally expressed by the rule that we must obey God rather than man. It is reflected in the use of the text of Jesus that: "You therefore are to be perfect, even as your heavenly Father is perfect" (Mt. 5:48). Vatican II describes this in the fifth chapter of *Lumen Gentium,* "The Call of the Whole Church to Holiness."[64] This chapter concludes by reminding Catholics that "those who make use of this world not get bogged down in it, for the structure of this world is passing away."[65] This means, from a religious perspective, that the claim of God and the values related to achieving union with God are of ultimate significance and constitute the highest moral claim on the individual. Theologically expressed, the Kingdom of God, a future event and the ultimate end of the person, is the highest value of the Roman Catholic and the obligatory nature of all other values must be discerned from their relation to the Kingdom of God. This ultimacy of the Kingdom in the Roman Catholic's value system does not condemn a position of solidarity with the world or imply a world-rejecting asceticism. Rather it keeps the Catholic from making the ideological mistake of calling "one concrete state in the development of human history the ultimate part."[66] Within a theology of the Kingdom, a Catholic can also affirm solidarity with the world while simultaneously criticizing "con-

[64] *Lumen Gentium,* quoted in Abbott, *The Documents of Vatican II, op. cit.,* pp. 65ff.

[65] *Ibid.,* p. 72

[66] Edward Schillebeeckx, *God, the Future of Man.* Trans. by N. D. Smith. (New York: Sheed and Ward, 1968), p. 186.

formity to the existing world as enraptured with its own appearance, and as concerned only with its self-glorification."[67]

The eschatological nature of the Church defines a major aspect of the Church's political and social role as one of critical negativity, "against every image of man whose lines are strictly drawn or which presents itself as a positive and total definition and against the illusory expectation that science and technology are capable of solving the ultimate problem of man's existence."[68] The Gospel contains a permanent criticism of any situation or institution simply because it is lacking in the qualities that make it a *total* human situation, that is, it is not the presence of the Kingdom. Schillebeeckx describes a twofold process: (1) the thrust of the Gospel provides a prophetic protest against humanity's limitations of the possibilities of its own existence with the result that a moral demand for change occurs; (2) the Gospel is to be formed into a responsible and concrete plan of action from a combination of theological and scientific analysis.[69] This methodology defines the indirect relation of the Gospel to social and political affairs, as well as the indirect relation between Church and society.

The Roman Catholic must approach all institutions (including the Church itself) as provisional and transitory and must acknowledge that the values proclaimed by all institutions are only approximate realizations of what will be. There is a crucial difference, though, between Church and State that implies the ethical necessity of a position of selective obedience to the State. The Church proclaims its own provisional character as part of its own inner nature. It cannot affirm that one state of its history is definitive.[70] This is because "the Church . . . will attain her full perfection only in heaven. Then will come the time of the restoration of all things."[71] Translated into

---

[67] Johannes B. Metz, *Theology of the World*. Trans. by William Glenn-Doepel. (New York: Herder and Herder, 1969), p. 92.

[68] Schillebeeckx, *God, the Future of Man, op. cit.*, p. 194.

[69] *Ibid.*, p. 159.

[70] Consult Thomas Love, *John Courtney Murray: Contemporary Church-State Theory, op. cit.*, pp. 146ff for an analysis of this position.

[71] *Lumen Gentium,* quoted in Abbott, *The Documents of Vatican II, op. cit.*, p. 78.

political categories, this means that the Church does not have a right to any vested interest in any situation, for its survival as an institution is not a primary value.[72] The Church does not have the right to make decisions on the basis of ideology because the *status quo* must and will pass away.

The political obligations of the Roman Catholic citizen must be understood and described in the light of this eschatological dimension of the Church. For the category of eschatology provides a broader basis for the analysis of traditional categories of political obligation, especially justice and the common good, by providing an ongoing critique of the actual state of justice in the society and the appropriation of the common good by all citizens. Justice and the common good, in the light of eschatology, may never be viewed as static concepts. Rather than functioning as legitimatizing principles of the *status quo,* the concepts of justice and the common good are to be defined not as existing realities, but as goals to be attained. The fact that Vatican II described the common good as dynamic[73] means that it should not be an ideology. When justice and the common good are not seen as achieved realities but as transcendent references for the ever continuing critical assessment of society, then the traditional position of the presumption of justice on the part of the State is weakened. The Roman Catholic citizen knows that the Kingdom has not arrived, that ideology can form a large part of the State's self-definition and political programs, and that, therefore, injustice is always present to some extent in contemporary reality. The obligation following from this is that the Roman Catholic citizen must exercise selectivity in giving allegiance to the State and its programs because it is not *a priori* certain that they are just in all respects.[74] The selectivity in obedience is directed primarily at

[72] This is not to imply that the Church as an institution has no value. It is to indicate that survival is not the issue, for the Church knows that it will not endure in whatever form it manifests at one particular time.

[73] *Gaudium et Spes,* quoted in Abbott, *The Documents of Vatican II, op. cit.,* p. 284.

[74] At this point, the analysis of Zahn would go further and suggest that it is safe to assume, *a priori,* that the programs of the State are not in conformity with the values of Roman Catholicism.

the specific programs and policies of the State and is based on whether or not these ensure the common good or, to state it another way, it is based on obedience to what the State should be. It may extend to the State itself if there is evidence of corruption and irresponsibility. To argue that a just procedural form of decision-making has been established, that all citizens have reasonable amounts of freedom, that the social and economic inequalities are equitably distributed and that most people have a good standard of living is not to guarantee either the justice of a particular policy or the quality of the standard of living. Therefore, selectivity in obedience to the State is required until the justice of the particular policy or action of the State is clearly demonstrated. The burden of proof is upon the State. The reason for this is that the Roman Catholic citizen knows that what the State does is provisional, can be laden with ideology and can be weighted on the side of a relatively unjust *status quo*. The justice of the State must be reasonably evident before the Catholic can obey.

The political obligation of a Roman Catholic citizen is qualified in the first instance by the eschatological nature of the Church which defines the provisional nature of all institutions. It is also qualified by the priority of the religious claims of the Church over the claims of the State. The religious claims of the Church relate its members to their ultimate destiny, life in the Kingdom of God. The claims of the State relate its members to participation in society so that their social needs may be fulfilled. Insofar as the goals and programs of a society are positively related to the development of the common good, the values of the State and Church may be in harmony and contribute to the growth of the Kingdom of God on earth.[75] But an examination must be conducted and a judgment made to discover if this is the case. Religious values which relate the individual to his or her ultimate end cannot be jeopardized through an uncritical presupposition of the justice of the State's cause. Selectivity in obedience is one principle which can be used in dealing with the tension between the values of the

---

[75] *Ibid.*, p. 237.

Church and State. This is not to argue that a Roman Catholic may act only with "pure" motives or that he or she cannot make compromises. In the framework described here, all actions will be only partial realizations of the values intended. What must be maintained, however, is that the Roman Catholic must discern whether or not the program or policy of the State contradicts or critically jeopardizes his or her religious values. In this analysis, the Roman Catholic must take into account the range of consequences that either obedience or disobedience will have. The consequences of the act must also be evaluated in terms of its effect on the individual, the Church and society, as well as on the formation of public opinion. The criterion of proportionality as well as the justice of the means must also play a part of this ethical evaluation. And such an evaluation will determine the Catholic citizen's action, which may range from vocal opposition to civil disobedience.[76]

The eschatological nature of the Church and the superiority of religious values provide the theological background and foundation for a doctrine of selective obedience to the State. A doctrine of selective obedience does not deny or minimize the reality or legitimacy of political obligations or the authority of the State. It attempts to discuss these obligations within the context of membership in other associations. The conclusion that has been drawn is that religious values, stemming from Church membership, are more ultimate and more binding than the values proposed by the State because religious values relate the individual to his or her destiny. The values of the State may help relate the individual to his or her ultimate destiny, but there is no necessary correlation between the values of the Church and the programs and policies set forth by the State. Selective obedience to the State maintains that before obeying the State, the Roman Catholic Church and its members have an obligation first to examine the justice of the State and its policies and to obey only if they do not contradict or jeopardize the realization of the more important religious values. Membership in the Church implies that the Roman Catholic must

---

[76] Consult Childress, *op. cit.*, pp. 169ff for the criteria for justifying civil disobedience.

observe and judge before he or she can act and they can act only when the values of the State positively contribute to the development of the common good of all and when the policies of the State do not clearly contradict religious values.

A principle such as selective obedience can have explosive consequences and implications, for there are problems with its application within a democratic society. Some of these problems have already been alluded to here; others have already found their way into the courts of the United States. An analysis of these problems provides another framework within which to analyze the principle of selective obedience within a democratic framework.

Chapter VI
From Principle to Practice

The purpose of this chapter is to examine the theory of selective obedience from the perspective of public policy. This examination will indicate areas and policies that are critical to some application of the general theory of selective obedience. To this end, the chapter will examine four areas: (1) general arguments against selective obedience; (2) selective conscientious objection to military service; (3) selective withholding of taxes; (4) two specific cases of selective obedience. The issues arising from these perspectives will help test the applicability of a general theory of selective obedience and will indicate the relevance of such a theory for the political processes.

A. General Problems with Selective Obedience

Although, as it has been developed in the foregoing chapters, the ethical principle of selective obedience finds a place within the structure of Roman Catholic thought on Church-Government relations and is based on ultimate loyalty to God and the eschatological nature of the Church, selective obedience may function as a disruptive principle within secular society, especially as this affects the decision-making processes of this society. The principle of selective obedience is properly seen as an explosive one, or one that can easily be applied to a wide variety of situations with the threat of disruption hovering in the background. Arguments have been indirectly raised against a general principle such as selective obedience in a discussion of the possibility of legitimating selective conscientious objection to the draft. Some of the arguments raised within this context are applicable to the general problem of selective obedience within a democratic society.

John Rohr[1] develops three major arguments that can be applied to selective objection. Stated briefly these are: (1) the presumption of the justice of the State; (2) the nature of representative democracy; and (3) the open-ended nature of selective obedience. Each of these will be discussed in turn.

In terms of the first argument, the presumption of justice, Rohr says that if such a presumption is not granted to the State, there would be no meaning to a description of the State as a moral community. Such selectivity as is claimed here could damage the common good which may call for obedience to an unjust law for the sake of preserving order or for attaining a specific end. Rohr argues that the existence of an unjust law does not *automatically* demand disobedience.[2]

Rohr himself inadvertently reveals the major weakness in the argument for the presumption of justice. He says, "In the absence of such a presumption the duty to obey legitimate authority would be drastically curtailed since the justice of so many decisions of public policy is often dubious."[3] The assertion of the dubious morality of public policy is the key to weakening the presumption of justice argument. Only *after* the arguments for the policy are fully spelled out can its morality be judged. For only then is it possible to examine both the procedural and substantive norms and arguments. An *a priori* presumption of justice could, in effect, imply a surrender of individual and corporate responsibility for moral decision-making to the State. It could also lead to a false separation of morality and politics in that ethical examination of public

---

[1] What follows are the writer's generalizations of arguments that Rohr uses against selective conscientious objection to war. Although Rohr does not address himself to the subject of this book, his arguments are valuable in that they raise problems generic to selective obedience. Consult Rohr, *Prophets Without Honor: Public Policy and Selective Conscientious Objection* (New York: Abingdon Press, 1971).

[2] *Ibid.*, p. 127.

[3] *Ibid.*, p. 117.

policy by citizens or other institutions would become unnecessary because the State and its laws are seen to possess their own conscience and the ability to make independent moral decisions.

The principle of selective obedience does not deny the proper autonomy of the State, its right to set public policy, and the seriousness of the political obligation of the citizen. Yet, in the case of the Catholic, selective obedience assures fidelity to religious claims because of their ultimacy. This, in turn, would imply an examination of the morality of public policy in order that the religious values of both the individual Church member and the religious institution itself will not be jeopardized through participation in a policy of dubious morality. In the selective obedience framework, neither obedience nor disobedience may be automatically presumed; what is presumed, even demanded, is an ethical examination of the policies of the State. The response of either obedience or disobedience will follow upon determination of the morality or immorality of the policy in question. The principle of selective obedience to the State requires an examination going beyond the merely strategic or political. For the Catholic, this principle implies that union with God, the priority of religious values, and the eschatological nature of the Church be taken seriously in discussing public policy to ensure that the policy ensures their fulfillment. The arguments from these religious premises may not be as inclusive as those based on grounds of public policy, but that neither invalidates them nor makes them untenable for the Church and its members must always give priority to their religious values. The reason for this is that in terms of examining the policies of the Government, both the Church and its individual members must look beyond ideological, political or strategic reasons to the religious values of the Church. Since membership in the Church implies a deeper and more lasting value commitment than that to the State, the Church and its members must, in the final analysis, be faithful to their religious values, even in their political dimensions. For while the spokes-persons for the arguments of public policy may present a firm case, these values are not the ultimate ones for the Church and its members. For these religious values are the ones that must determine or qualify their actions.

The principle of selective obedience challenges the tradition of the *a priori* presumption of the justice of the State's actions because of religious claims which are more ultimate and which are more binding on the individual and the Church. It imposes an ethical investigation and evaluation of the State's policy in recognition of the fact that the values of the Church and State are not always the same and the possibility that the State's argument rests upon ideology must be taken into account. The morality of the State's actions is not denied by this principle, but rather is qualified by the religious demands placed upon some of its citizens who are members of the Roman Catholic Church. Selective obedience takes seriously political obligations and the necessity of fulfilling the requirements of the common good. It insists, however, that the implications of this type of responsibility require a more rigorous examination of public policy so that the more ultimate and significant religious claims will not be jeopardized or ignored.

Rohr's second argument suggests that if the Government must seek the consent of the governed on every issue, representative democratic structures have no meaning. Rohr would argue that, instead of having a referendum for every governmental decision, the Government would meet the norms of the consent of the governed by (1) being duly elected and (2) enjoying widespread support for its policies.[4] The principle of selective obedience, rightly understood, does not seek to deny the validity of representative Government, nor does it imply a need for incessant referenda. All that it does imply is that the citizen may not surrender his or her conscience to the Government. That the Government has been duly elected and a majority of citizens support its policies does not guarantee the justice of the policy.

Selective obedience requires that although the religious values of the citizen and the values and policies of the State interpenetrate and can be a source of tension for the Catholic

---

[4] *Ibid.*, pp. 147-48.

citizen because of these competing claims, nevertheless the State is not free to determine *a priori* what may or may not be claimed as a religious value.[5] This is the area in which radical religious freedom must be demanded and granted, although the claims for religious values must be tested in terms both of the religious tradition and of their effect on public policy. It is instructive to recall here the strong statement of Vatican II.

This freedom means that all men are to be immune from coercion on the part of individuals or of social groups and of any human power, in such wise that in matters religious no one is to be forced to act in a manner contrary to his own beliefs. Nor is anyone to be restrained from acting in accordance with his own beliefs, whether privately or in association with others, within due limits.[6]

Within the context of selective obedience, this statement means that, from a religious perspective, no Catholic who is a citizen can be forced to participate in actions judged by the individual or the Church to be immoral. It strongly implies the necessity of investigating and evaluating policies to see if they are in harmony with one's beliefs. The statement goes on to distinguish between the *right* to resist and the *duty* to resist in saying that although one has the right to refrain from action, there is no necessary duty to act, or, if action is taken, due limits must be observed. The important point remains, however, that neither duly elected officials nor a majority of citizens, acting in support of governmental policies, have any right to coerce the individual into acting against his or her beliefs, within due limits such as proportionality, the safeguarding of the rights of all citizens, and the just requirements of the public order.

A third argument of Rohr against selective objection is that it knows no limits, or as Ralph Potter expresses the argument: "To admit an absolute right of an individual to withdraw with

---

[5] Ralph Potter, "Conscientious Objection to Particular Wars," quoted in Donald A. Giannella, ed., *Religion and the Public Order*, Vol. 4. (Ithaca: Cornell University Press, 1968), p. 87.

[6] *Dignitas Humanae*, quoted in Abbott, *The Documents of Vatican II, op. cit.,* pp. 678-79.

utter impunity from participation in actions obnoxious to his political, moral or religious sensitivities would be to invite anarchy."[7] Potter is referring specifically to the issue of objection to war but he fears that if the principle were allowed in one area, it could and would be extended to all other areas of civil life, e.g., taxation.[8] The theory of selective obedience is the generalized form of this position, stated in affirmative terms. Defined in this way, selective obedience is a premise of ethical behavior that must be operative in all segments of political evaluation done by the Catholic citizen. It suggests that all aspects of political life, and certainly those of serious matter, must be examined in the light of religious and ethical principles before obedience to these policies can be given. It is a serious reminder to the Catholic citizen that political behavior must be in conformity with religious values and that when there is conflict, priority must always be given to the religious values because of their ultimacy.

Does this principle lead to anarchy? It could, but only if: (1) the Government proves itself totally insensitive to moral issues, (2) the majority of citizens are not informed as to the issues of the day, (3) the Government's policies were based only on ideology rather than the common good, (4) there were no means of reform within the system, and (5) there is no appeal to right reason or responsible argumentation. It must be remembered that selective obedience is a theory of *obedience,* which is recognized normally as part of one's political obligations; but the obedience owed to the State is *selective* in that it is informed by religious values and concern for the common good and supported by a critical, ethical evaluation of public policy. The fear of anarchy may be legitimately raised in opposition to selective obedience only when the Government

---

[7] Ralph Potter, "Conscientious Objection to Particular Wars," *op. cit.,* p. 87.

[8] This was one of the major reasons the National Advisory Commission on Selective Service argued against the legalization of selective objection to war. The fear was that it would open the door to a general theory of selective disobedience, which would destroy society. Consult *In Pursuit of Equity: Who Serves When Not All Serve?* (Washington, D. C.: U. S. Government Printing Office, 1967), pp. 50-51.

is at such a low moral level, that if not anarchy, at least a radical change in Government could be an appropriate response. Selective obedience would pose a serious threat to Government only when there is a question of unethical Governmental policies. In this sense, it could perform a positive function for the Government and the common good by reminding the Government that its policies will be scrutinized and tested in the light of ethical and religious principles.

The principle of selective obedience to the State, therefore, takes seriously the nature of political obligation and responsibility to the common good. It demands, however, the examination of political decisions in the light of religious commitment because of the ultimacy of these values. Obedience will be given, qualified or refused in proportion to the degree of harmony and conformity between public policy and religious belief. It would exclude as utterly inappropriate to Christian belief and demeaning to the Christian citizen the kind of automatic and unquestioning obedience the State has come to take for granted under the "presumption of justice" interpretation of civil responsibility.

B. Selective Conscientious Objection to War: Case Study 1

The rise of the phenomenon of selective conscientious objection (SCO) or objection to particular wars provides an occasion for an examination of an application of the general theory of selective obedience to a particular situation. Several cases of SCO have been brought to court and the arguments presented provide a basis for an analysis on legal as well as moral or theological grounds.

The example of SCO is particularly applicable to this book because the American Roman Catholic Bishops have endorsed the legitimacy and morality of this position in their pastoral letter "Human Life in Our Day" (15 November 1968). The bishops base their reasoning on the fact that selective conscientious dissent frequently "reflects the influence of the principle which informs modern papal teaching, the Pastoral Constitution and a classic tradition of moral doctrine in the Church, including, in fact, the norms for the moral evaluation of a theoretically just war."[9] In the light of this and the suggestion of Vatican II that humane provision be given to conscientious objectors to war, the American Bishops recommend

a modification of the Selective Service Act making it possible, although not easy, for so-called selective conscientious objectors to refuse—without fear of imprisonment or loss of citizenship —to serve in wars which they consider unjust or in branches of service (e.g., the strategic nuclear forces) which would subject them to the performance of actions contrary to deeply held moral convictions about indiscriminate killing.[10]

Although neither this pastoral letter nor the later statement of the United States Catholic Conference "Declaration on Conscientious Objection and Selective Conscientious Objection" (21 October 1971) presents a detailed argument for the SCO position, these statements do accept the primacy of conscience and the validity of the SCO position in Catholic morality, and stress the necessity and importance of legitimating the SCO through a change in the Selective Service Act. As the United States Catholic Conference expressed it: "In the light of the Gospel and from an analysis of the Church's teaching on conscience, it is clear that a Catholic can be a conscientious objector to war in general or to a particular war 'because of religious training and belief.' "[11] For the Catholic, then the problem of the SCO is important because it reveals a very real tension between Church and State.

Three sources are employed here for examination: the Report of the National Advisory Commission on Selective Service, court cases that have an indirect relation to SCO, and court cases specifically dealing with the SCO.

---

[9] "Human Life in Our Day," Pastoral Letter of the American Catholic Hierarchy (Washington, D. C.: United States Catholic Conference, 15 November 1968), p. 43.

[10] *Ibid.*, p. 44.

[11] "Declaration on Conscientious Objection and Selective Conscientious Objection," United States Catholic Conference, 21 October 1971.

In 1967, a presidential commission was established to study the selective service system. One section of its report deals specifically with SCO and presents five arguments against it which led the commission to reject it. The arguments are summarized as follows: (1) The majority felt that the status of the conscientious objector is properly applied only to those opposed to all killing under any circumstances. The reason for this is that it is one thing to deal in law with a person, responding to a moral principle outside of the person which opposes all killing; it is another thing to grant special privileges to those who believe that there is a moral imperative telling the individual that he or she can kill in some circumstances and not in others. (2) The majority held that selective pacifism is essentially a political question of support or nonsupport of national policy and cannot be judged in terms of special moral imperatives. (3) It was argued that this position could open the door to a general theory of selective disobedience to law which could destroy the fabric of Government. The commission noted that opposition to a particular war could lead to opposition to paying a particular tax. (4) The commission could not see the morality of a proposition which would permit the selective pacifist to avoid combat through a program of alternate service in support of a war which he had concluded was unjust. (5) Finally, it was argued that a recognition of SCO could be disruptive to the morale and effectiveness of the armed forces. A determination of the justice or injustice of the war could be made only within the context of the war. This would put a burden on the person in uniform by forcing upon this individual the necessity of making such a decision because the Government's obligation to do this for the person would be taken away.[12]

In response to this position, it should be noted first of all that the commission did not present detailed arguments to support their position. The report confuses the issue somewhat by referring to the SCO as a selective pacifist. This is the point

---

[12] *In Pursuit of Equity: Who Serves When Not All Serve?, op. cit.,* pp. 50-51.

at issue: The SCO is *not* an absolute pacifist for this individual is willing to fight and kill—but only in a just war.[13] The commission, in its final argument, seems to confuse the possibility of a decline in morale with an actual occurrence of such an event. No evidence is presented to support the likelihood of such an event occurring. This same argument also indicates that the Government may be suspicious of the individual conscience or at least that it does not want to extend too far the rights of that conscience into the political area. The commission does not see what type of alternate service the SCO could perform. If the SCO's were given the same options that conscientious objectors are, this would not be an issue. The SCO is not necessarily arguing that the Government itself is unjust, but only that a specific act of the Government is. Alternate service, therefore, which would be supportive of the Government or contributory to the common good would not necessarily be morally repulsive to the conscience of the SCO. The commission argues that the position of the SCO is a political, not a moral, position. Here the commission directly opposes traditionally Roman Catholic teaching on the just war and in particular the argument of the American Catholic hierarchy that SCO is a morally unjustifiable stance in accordance with tradition and Vatican II. A position such as that of the commission introduces a false distinction between politics and morality for it implicitly argues that empirical data, which may be political, should not be included in moral reasoning. This is also indirectly indicated by the Government's insistence that the traditional conscientious objector is apolitical because this person condemns all wars and not an action or policy of a specific Government. Again, such an argument contradicts Roman Catholic moral tradition and the specific directive of Vatican II to avoid assuming a separation between civil and religious life.[14] The effect of assuming the correctness of the

---

[13] A somewhat broader variation of this position is represented by the Catholic who accepts the just war position as theologically sound, but insists that no modern war can meet the criteria of the just war. This position, while essentially "selective," would be functionally pacifist.

[14] *Gaudium et Spes,* quoted in Abbott, *op. cit.,* p. 243.

commission's argument could be to separate conscience from politics and would, in the long run, reduce religious institutions to "sacristy churches," or purely "other-worldly" institutions, which description does not apply to the Roman Catholic Church. The only argument that the commission makes that is genuinely relevant is that the legitimation of SCO could easily be generalized and applied to other areas of national life. This is the precise point of the theory of selective obedience, which affirms legitimate obedience to legitimate authority. A response to this argument has been presented earlier in this chapter; it can be noted here that this hypothetical situation would happen only if there were serious questions about the morality of the Government in all dimensions. And if such were the case, the common good would justify the removal of such a Government. The position of SCO is threatening to the Government because one of its crucial powers is being questioned. Yet if the Government is free to disregard such challenges, what becomes of democracy and the rights of conscience? If the Government position cannot withstand such a challenge or test, what is to be thought of the correctness—let alone the morality—of its cause?

Some cases have been brought to court that have an indirect bearing on the problem of SCO because of the principles stated in them. One of these is *U.S. v. Macintosh*.[15] Macintosh was a Canadian who, in 1931, applied for naturalization. His petition was refused because: "He is unwilling to leave the question of his future military service to the wisdom of the Congress where it belongs, and where every native born or admitted citizen is obliged to leave it."[16] Macintosh had qualified his oath to defend the Constitution by force of arms with the proviso that the war had to be morally justified. Because of this he was, in effect, claiming the right to be a SCO at some future time. The reasoning of the Court on this point is instructive.

But also we are a Nation whose Constitution contemplates war as well as peace; whose government must go forward on the

---

[15] *U.S. v. Macintosh,* 283 U.S. 605.
[16] *Ibid.,* 624.

assumption, and safely can proceed upon no other, that unqualified allegiance to the Nation and submission and obedience
to the laws of the land, as well as those made for war as those
made for peace, are not inconsistent with the will of God.[17]

This position of the Court directly contradicts a major
premise of Christianity, and Roman Catholicism in particular.
Unqualified allegiance to the nation is inconsistent with the will
of God because this would equate the State with God and
would be idolatry. This position also denies the rights of conscience and the right to freedom of religion which states that
no one can be coerced to perform acts against his or her
conscience.[18] As such, this position represents an affront to
Christianity and the rights of conscience.

Another case is that of *Hamilton v. Regents of the University of California*.[19] Hamilton contended that the University
requirement of compulsory training in military science infringed
upon the liberty guaranteed by the 14th Amendment. In deciding the case, which Hamilton lost, the Court made two
observations of importance for my argument. The first was
that acts indirectly related to military service are not so tied
to the practice of religion that they are exempt in law or morals
from regulation by the State.[20] The second is the statement
that

The conscientious objector, if his liberties were to be extended,
might refuse to contribute taxes in furtherance of a war, whether
for attack or defense, or in furtherance of any end condemned
by his conscience as irreligious or immoral. The right of private
judgment has never yet been so exalted above the power and
the compulsion of the agencies of the government.[21]

Roman Catholic moral theology has distinguished between
direct and indirect cooperation in acts that are immoral. This
distinction points out that acts which the court considered

---

[17] *Ibid.,* 625.
[18] *Dignitas Humanae,* quoted in Abbott, *op. cit.,* p. 678.
[19] *Hamilton v. Regents of the University of California,* 293 U.S. 245.
[20] *Ibid.,* 267.
[21] *Ibid.,* 268.

indirectly related to service in the armed forces are a concern of religion and therefore the Catholic must resolve the issue of indirect cooperation with a possibly immoral action or policy before engaging in it. While it is possible for casuistry to gain the upper hand here, still, it would be impossible to deny that an examination of indirect cooperation is a part of Catholic moral teaching.

The form of both arguments of the Court suggest that tradition is to be the final arbiter of the rights of conscience and the power of the State. To argue that a position is incorrect because it has never been advanced is not to argue against the position itself. It may be the case that, in the face of the expanding power of the Government, now is the precise moment to argue for and insist on the rights of the individual. Although the rights of the majority must always be protected and hold their rightful position, still we may not automatically presume that whatever the majority decides or supports is correct from a moral point of view. There is an area of tension between the rights of the majority and the minority; the tension is not resolved, however, by a suspension of judgment. What is required is an analysis of the argument as well as the consequences of the policy.

The case of *U.S. v. Kurki*[22] is noteworthy in that the Court declared that it had no authority to create a classification for a particular war pacifist. All this decision did was to reaffirm that this power is proper to the Congress. In *U.S. v. Mitchell*[23] the Court distinguished the Congressional power to raise and support armies from the use the Executive makes of such armies. The Court thereupon refused to consider this dimension of Executive power. "Thus we need not consider whether the substantive issues raised by appellant can ever be appropriate for judicial determination."[24] Because of this, the issues involved in the SCO classification were not allowed to be argued.

The combined case of *Gillette v. U.S. and Negre v. Larsen*[25]

---

[22] *U.S. v. Kurki*, 255 F. Supp. 161.
[23] *U.S. v. Mitchell*, 359 F. Supp. 2d 323.
[24] *Ibid.*, 323.
[25] *Gillette v. U.S.*, 91 S. Ct. 828.

is the only court case dealing with the specific issues involved in SCO. Basically the Supreme Court held that objectors to particular wars are not within the purview of the traditional exemption for conscientious objectors even though these objections are rooted in conscience and are religious in nature. The Court therefore ruled that Section 6(j)[26] of the Selective Service Act of 1967 "does not violate the establishment clause on theory that it works a de facto discrimination against religions nor does it violate the free exercise clause by conscripting persons who oppose a particular war on the grounds of conscience and religion."[27]

In rendering this decision, the Court used three arguments. The first argument is that Section 6(j) applies only to total objectors. This is based mainly on the argument that there is no basis to the claim that Congress intended in this section to recognize any conscientious claim whatsoever to relieve a person from military service.[28] The argument is that if Section 6(j) exempts only total objectors, that is what the exemption means and no other interpretation is to be placed on it.

The second argument against Gillette is that Section 6(j) does not violate the establishment clause of the First Amendment. There are three reasons for this. (1) Section 6(j) does not discriminate on the basis of religious affiliation or belief and the petitioners have not shown the absence of a neutral, secular basis for the exemption. The Court argues that 6(j) does not single out any religious organization or creed for special treatment. The hopelessness of converting a sincere conscientious objector into an effective fighting man, the State's recognition of the duty due a moral power higher than the State, and the concern for the hard choice that conscription would impose on a conscientious objector constitute valid secu-

---

[26] Section 6(j) states in part that "Nothing contained in this title shall be construed to require any person to be subject to combatant training and service in the Armed Forces of the United States who, by reason of religious training and belief is conscientiously opposed to participation in war in any form." *Handbook for Conscientious Objectors* (Philadelphia: The Larchwood Press, Inc., 1970), p. 29.

[27] *Gillette v. U.S.*, 91 S. Ct. 828.

[28] *Ibid.*, 834.

lar purposes, which are also neutral, for the exemption in 6(j).
Besides, Gillette did not show that these are religious reasons,
and thus his argument does not stand.[29] (2) The exemption
focuses on individual conscientious belief and not on sectarian
affiliation. The exemption, therefore, does not encourage membership in traditional peace churches. The dilemma of the
SCO arises because of personal conscientious objection.[30] (3)
There are valid, neutral reasons, with central emphasis on fairness in the administration of military conscription, for limiting
the exemption to total objectors. Many reasons support this
claim of the Court. One is the obvious need to provide manpower for fighting wars. The problem of maintaining a fair
system for determining who serves when not all serve constitutes a significant argument for the Court. The problem is that
SCO is a claim of uncertain dimensions and to grant it could
promote erratic or discriminatory decision-making. The claim
for SCO is subjective and attaining fairness in evaluating such
claims would be difficult. The Court indicates that it is possible
that the objector who is more articulate, better educated, or
better counseled would be the one to obtain such an exemption
and therefore objectors not having these advantages would be
at a disadvantage. There could also be danger of an unintended
religious discrimination in that the more a claim corresponded
to a conventional religion, the better chance of success it would
have. The Court felt that the traditional limitation of Section
6(j) served as an over-riding interest in protecting the integrity
of democratic decision-making against claims to individual
non-compliance. The problem of using SCO as a wedge to
open the door to other forms of selective disobedience and the
possibility of an SCO exemption weakening the resolve of those
who feel bound to serve in the armed forces are other reasons
why the Court suggests limiting the claim to total objectors.
And finally, the Court argues that if it would appear that those
who fight are chosen unfairly, a mood of bitterness might arise

---

[29] *Ibid.,* 837-38.

[30] *Ibid.,* 838.

which would corrode the spirit of willingly performing public service.[31]

The third major argument against Gillette is that Section 6(j) does not violate the Free Exercise clause of the First Amendment. The two reasons for this are that the conscription laws are not designed to interfere with any religious practice nor do they work a penalty against any theological position and that the incidental burdens felt by the SCO are justified by substantial Governmental interests.

These arguments are the Government's case against SCO. They have been judged by the Supreme Court as compelling enough to reject a claim for selective conscientious objection. There are, however, some problematic areas in these arguments.

One presentation of these problems is found in *U.S. v. McFadden*.[32] McFadden, a Roman Catholic, applied for conscientious objector status on the grounds that he considered the Vietnam war to be unjust. In the United States District Court, Northern District California, Justice Zerpoli held "that statute exempting from military service only those persons whose religious beliefs forbade them to participate in war in any form placed such a burden upon religious beliefs of Catholic selective objectors so as to violate the free exercise clause of the First Amendment."[33] Although this case was taken to the Supreme Court where judgment was vacated and the case was remanded to the United States District Court of the Northern District of California[34] and has not, as of this writing, been ruled on, nevertheless, the arguments presented here are important and deserve consideration.

The basic argument of *McFadden* is that Section 6(j) puts him in the unconstitutional choice of violating a cardinal principle of his religion or suffer the consequence of jail and/or a fine.

The Court argued that choosing fidelity to religion by not participating in an unjust war would place upon McFadden

---

[31] *Ibid.*, 839-41
[32] *U.S. v. McFadden*, 309 F. Supp. 502 (1970).
[33] *Loc. cit.*
[34] 401 U.S. 1006.

the burden of a possible five-year jail sentence and a possible $10,000 fine. This burden of a criminal penalty is placed upon the Catholic selective objector. The Court quotes from Chief Justice Stone: "Compelling the citizen to refrain from doing an act which he regards as moral and conscientious does not do violence to his conscience: but his conscience is violated if he is coerced into doing an act which is opposed to his deepest convictions of right and wrong."[35] If, therefore, the Selective Service statute does not exempt the Catholic selective objector, it violates this prohibition against the State's commanding one to act against one's conscience. The point here is that if Congress grants an exemption to some, it cannot deny it to others based on unconstitutional grounds.

The Court also argued that 6(j) "clearly discriminates between those who are opposed to all wars on religious grounds and those who are opposed to particular wars on religious grounds."[36] The reason for this is that "when the law which affects primary rights draws a distinction between classes that distinction must be supported by a compelling state interest."[37] The Court declared that possible efficiency in the administration of 6(j) is not a compelling reason for denying a SCO classification to Catholics.

The Court suggests three possible justifications for such discrimination against Catholics. The first is that removing the phrase "war in any form" from 6(j) would result in a substantial loss of manpower. The Court suggests that the same argument was used against the removal of the requirement of belief in a Supreme Deity and notes that the projected losses in manpower never occurred. And, in connection with this, the Court indicated that means are available for resolving any such decrease in manpower. "In the area of primary freedoms the government is required to show that no alternate means exist to satisfy the governmental interest."[38] The Court notes that by 1980 there will be eighteen and one-half million

---

[35] *U.S. v. McFadden*, 309 F. Supp. 505.
[36] *Ibid.*, 506.
[37] *Ibid.*, 507.
[38] *Loc. cit.*

(18,500,000) men of draft age; the revoking of college defer-ments is mentioned as a possibility as well as reminding us that there are over two million men in active and stand-by reserves. Because alternate means exist, there is no compelling governmental interest in maintaining the present law without exempting SCO's.

The second argument is that exempting men such as Mc-Fadden will endanger the morale of the troops. But the argu-ment also goes the other way. A man drafted in opposition to deep-seated convictions will not make a good soldier and will endanger the morale of the troops.

The final argument for such discrimination is that exten-sion of the exemption to all selective religious objectors would open the door to all types of spurious claims. In arguing against this, the Court notes that such an argument was rejected in another case.[39] Justice Zirpole also quotes from the Sisson case (297 F. Supp. 901, 909): "Seeger cut the ground from under that argument. So does experience. . . . The suggestion that the court cannot tell a sincere from an insincere conscientious objector underestimates what the judicial process performs every day."[40] The Court concluded this stage of the argument by stating that there was no compelling State interest which would justify discrimination against Catholic selective objectors.

The Court also found that such discrimination violates the establishment of religion clause of the First Amendment in that it prefers pacifist religions over non-pacifist religions. Citations from two previous cases for the arguments for this: (1) *Everson v. Board of Education* (330 U.S. 1): "Neither a state nor the Federal Government can set up a Church. Neither can pass laws which aid one religion, aid all religions or prefer

---

[39] *Sherbert v. Verner,* 374 U.S. 398. In this case, the Court rejected a South Carolina statute which denied unemployment compensation to a Seventh-Day Adventist because she refused without good cause to ac-cept suitable work when offered. The reason for her conscientious re-fusal to work was the prohibition by her religion to work on Saturday. The Court declared this infringement of her free exercise of religion could be justified only on the basis of compelling State interest, which was not demonstrated.

[40] *U.S. v. McFadden,* 309 F. Supp. 508.

one religion over another." (2) *Epperson v. Arkansas* (393 U.S. 97): "Government in our democracy, state and national, must be neutral in matters of religious theory, doctrine, and practice. . . . It may not aid, foster, or promote one religion or religious theory against another. . . ."[41]

McFadden makes a strong point which was assumed in *Gillette:* compelling Government interest. The Court stated, in *Gillette,* that there were compelling State interests for not granting the exemption to SCO's. These interests were not presented in the arguments and this omission constitutes a severe weakness in the case.[42] In *Gillette,* the Government argues that the current exemption represented valid secular purposes. Although this is a valid argument in itself, it does not provide a basis for indicating a compelling State interest. Such interest in a case this serious must be directly and clearly indicated, not assumed or declared present by Government decree.

The argument for fairness in the system of conscription used by the Government in *Gillette* is hypothetical in that it suggests what could happen if the SCO exemption were to be granted. The possibility of erratic decision-making could be partially resolved by careful definitions within the law itself and also by demanding review boards whose members are competent. This could require training sessions and education in the just war theory or other religious and non-religious claims for SCO. And, if discrimination should result, the courts are available to hear appeals, as they have been for problems with the present law. Difficulties are present in terms of extending 6(j) to selective objectors, but they are not insurmountable—at least the Government has not presented reasons as to why they are.

Another reason, used in *Gillette,* for the rejection of SCO is the variety of reasons that could be given as the basis for such objections. This argument indicates a lack of awareness of just war theory. Part of the responsibility for this may be on the part of the Churches which have shied away from ap-

---

[41] *Ibid,* 508.
[42] *Gillette v. U.S.,* 91 S. Ct. 842.

plications of it as well as from developing the theory in relation to modern warfare. Yet the fact remains that there are basic norms for the just war theory and while some factors may tend to be subjective from the perspective of the Government, there are enough objective norms to provide an adequate judgment on the justice or injustice of the war.[43] The majority of these norms provide enough of a basis for objectivity to undercut the Governmental assertions that the SCO claim is subjective.

The argument that the better counseled and educated and more articulate objector would be more likely to receive such an exemption is really not applicable because it holds equally well for the present exemption of the total objector. The same could possibly be said of the Government's argument that the objector belonging to a more traditional religion would be more likely to receive the exemption. Until *Welch,* only the traditional theist could obtain the exemption—clearly a type of religious discrimination.

The argument is also advanced that an SCO exemption would open the door to a general theory of selective disobedience to law. The most serious weakness of this argument is that it assumes as a fact what the argument proposes as an hypothesis. Because such a theory may arise does not mean that it will arise; no factual conclusions may be drawn from an hypothetical argument. Nor does the Government provide reasons to show why such a theory would arise if the new exemption were granted. This argument rests on assumptions and on the fear of anarchy. Disobedience to unjust laws does not promote anarchy; rather it is part of the American tradition to resist such laws, a tradition to which the Court itself refers. Legitimate dissent within a society can contribute to the health of that society by exposing injustices which could destroy the country. Instead of being fearful of a general

---

[43] For a listing of such norms, consult Liane Norman, "Selective Conscientious Objection," *The Center Magazine* (May/June, 1972), p. 19. For an analysis from a Catholic perspective, consult Gordon Zahn, "Religion and War," Newman Review (Spring, 1963), reprinted in Zahn, *War, Conscience, and Dissent, op. cit.,* pp. 75ff.

theory of selective obedience, it would be more prudent to fear a Government which attempts to suppress legitimate dissent which has objective reasoning as well as fidelity to religious values at its foundation.

As of this writing, the Government, acting through the Supreme Court, has refused to grant exemption to selective conscientious objectors to war. This is a rejection of a specific application of a general theory of selective obedience. The arguments presented by the Government and sanctioned by the Court are not in themselves irrefutable. They are based on assumptions of what could happen if such an exemption were granted without providing reasons to support such an hypothesis. There is also a definite need for the Government to indicate what compelling State interests would be jeopardized by granting such an exemption. Up until now, these reasons have been assumed; now they must be made perfectly clear if the argument is to have any weight. There is also the possibility of religious discrimination against a Roman Catholic because the Church to which he or she belongs holds the just war theory instead of total pacifism. As a result the individual is in the position of choosing to offend his or her conscience or facing a criminal penalty for being true to his or her religious responsibilities.

C. Tax Resistance: Case Study 2

A second form of resistance to war that has been receiving growing attention and participation calls for withholding part or all of either the excise tax imposed on telephone service[44] or the federal income tax. This is a type of civilian conscientious objection to war because all can participate in it, not only those men of draft age. As a form of resistance, its purpose

[44] In April 1966, Congress raised the excise tax on telephone service to 10%. This tax is directly related to the funding of the Vietnam war. Consult *Ain't Gonna Pay for War No More,* Robert Calvert, ed. Published by War Tax Resistance, 34 Lafayette St., New York, N. Y. 10012.

is to oppose the war-making power of the nation-state by refusing to finance war or war-related activities.

The tax resistance movement is directed to action; for this reason, the vast majority of the literature on this movement is programmatic or informational. One of the main handbooks, *Ain't Gonna Pay for War No More,* provides information on the injustice of the Vietnam war, types of legal penalties involved, and the personal example of different resisters. The newsletters, *The Peacemaker* and *Final Draft-Only for Life,* fulfill this same purpose, as well as providing information on new cases of resistance. As an explanation of their action, tax resisters simply argue that the Vietnam war is unjust, the paying of taxes to support it is an immoral form of cooperation in evil and therefore tax monies must be withheld or channeled to other purposes or funds. The courts, needless to say, have not given any support to this type of resistance, nor has the Internal Revenue Service looked upon this with favor. In effect, the resistance does little more than slow down the collection process, since the Government can simply attach liens to property, checking or savings accounts to obtain the money. But the point of non-voluntary cooperation is made.

One dimension of this movement has been the proposal to establish a World Peace Tax Fund, introduced in the Congress on 17 April 1972 by Representative Dellums of California.[45] This bill, H.R. 14414, proposes that

a taxpayer conscientiously opposed to participation in war may elect to have his income, estate or gift tax payments spent for non-military purposes; to create a Trust Fund (The World Peace Tax Fund) to receive these payments; to establish a World Peace Tax Fund Board of Directors; and for other purposes.[46]

This act would establish a conscientious objector status,

---

[45] "World Peace Tax Fund Act." *Congressional Record,* Vol. 118, no. 59, 17 April 1972. Citations of this Act are taken from the reprint of it issued by the WPTF Steering Committee, Box 1447, Ann Arbor, Michigan 48106. The writer would like to thank Mrs. Elizabeth Boardman of the Cambridge office of the American Friends Service Committee for making this and other information on tax resistance available.

[46] World Peace Tax Fund Act, p. 1 of mimeographed text.

parallel to that now provided under the Selective Service Act, for those persons who cannot, in good conscience, contribute to military expenditures and provides the option of alternate payments comparable to the alternative service option now available to those who reject military service. Persons claiming such an exemption from military contributions would be certified as conscientious objectors by the Selective Service System and any taxpayer "who declares that he or she is conscientiously opposed to participation in war, within the meaning of the Military Selective Service Act"[47] would qualify. This status would be obtained through an indication of such objection on the tax form and would be subject to challenge in the U.S. District Courts.

The Act would recognize that participation in war through the payment of taxes can be as morally repugnant as participation through active service in the armed forces. The Act proposes a legal alternative which, while it does not deny the citizen's duty to pay taxes, would recognize his or her moral responsibility for the uses to which his or her tax monies would be put. The Act, in short, provides for a legitimate, constructive use of dissent from uses of tax monies deemed immoral.

One weakness of the bill is that one must be opposed to participation in war in all forms; like the present military conscription program, it does not take into account the many people who may object to a particular war. We are faced here with the same problem described above: for Roman Catholics, for whom selective objection is a moral obligation, even such indirect cooperation in an unjust war could be at least materially sinful.[48] Again there is the reality of a violation

---

[47] *Ibid.*, p. 1.

[48] Cooperation is generally defined as "any and every physical or moral assistance in the commission of a sinful action in union with others." This may be formal (cooperation in the sin of another which by inner purpose or deliberate intent is perceived as complicity in the sin of another) or material (a good or indifferent act which contributes to the sin of another by being misused or misappropriated by this person and placed in the service of his sinful activity). If a Catholic believed a particular war to be unjust, it would obviously be formal cooperation to contribute taxes to finance it. If there were doubt about the justice of

of religious freedom in forcing a group of people to perform actions morally repugnant to their conscience.

To counter the argument that this Act would introduce anarchy, the authors of the Act present a rationale demonstrating the soundness of the bill, along with several precedents. This writer is of the opinion that these arguments would also hold were the bill to be extended to selective objectors.

First, the Act does *not* advocate the nonpayment of taxes. Instead, the Act reaffirms the duty of taxation and provides for an alternate distribution of the tax monies. Secondly, there are already instances where tax exemptions protect religious and conscientious belief. Section 1420(e) of the present law exempts from payment of self-employment taxes ministers, members of religious orders, or Christian Science practitioners who are conscientiously opposed to participation in an insurance plan such as that proposed by the Social Security Act. Section 1402(h) relieves members of qualified religious faiths, primarily the Amish, of the duty to pay Social Security taxes. These exemptions have established a principle of Congressional accommodation to conscientious beliefs in the area of taxation. The World Peace Tax Fund Act could be another application of this accommodation. The Act's sponsors argue that, following recent Court decisions—especially *Sherbert v. Verner*—such a provision is an accommodation for the free exercise of religion, not an establishment thereof.[49]

Although this Act deals only with traditional conscientious objectors, and has yet to stand the test of examination by various House committees, it holds promise of a meaningful

---

the war, the cooperation could be material and the act of paying taxes could also be indifferent. But, in this connection, it is well to note that Bernard Haering, a leading contemporary Catholic moral theologian, is of the opinion that a clerk in a store which sells birth control pills is guilty of formally cooperating in sin by selling them to a customer; this clerk is also obliged to quit this job and find new employment. Haering also mentions that the duty of obedience to one's employer does not excuse the clerk from sin. One wonders why equally strict moral judgments concerning formal cooperation in sin are not made about either participation in or cooperation with war or the armed forces. Consult Bernard Haering, *The Law of Christ,* Vol. II, *op. cit.,* pp. 495-517.

[49] World Peace Tax Fund Act, pp. 3-4 in mimeographed text.

advance in political participation of the citizen by giving him or her moral responsibility for determining where certain tax monies will not go. It also helps strengthen the American tradition of dissent and yet puts this dissent to remarkably good use by both insisting on the duty to pay taxes and by allowing a portion of that money to be used to promote peace activities. If it does not yet allow for selectivity in objection to war, as full recognition of the principle of selective obedience would require, it does promote the principle of selectivity by recognizing that when people are totally opposed to war, it is a violation of their religious freedom to force them to pay taxes to support the war.

D. Catholic Resistance in Nazi Germany: Case Study 3

Although the record of the Catholic Church in Nazi Germany was largely one of conformity and compromise, there were many examples of heroic individual resistance which can serve as examples of selective obedience to the State. Two such examples are found in the behavior of Franz Jaegerstaetter, an Austrian peasant executed for conscientious objection, and Bishop von Galen, noted for his opposition to the euthanasia program.

Jaegerstaetter's full story has been documented by Gordon Zahn.[50] After a somewhat capricious youth, Jaegerstaetter settled down, married and lived an exceptionally devout Catholic life. As the Nazi power grew more total, so did Jaegerstaetter's resistance to it. He voted against the German annexation of Austria and refused to contribute the funds collected to support Nazi sponsored organizations. In addition, he refused to accept the benefits offered by the Government for families and cash subsidies for poor crops.[51] He also refused to let family responsibilities deter him from fulfilling his religious obligations

---

[50] Gordon Zahn, *In Solitary Witness* (New York: Holt, Rinehart and Winston, 1964).

[51] *Ibid.*, pp. 46-50.

and he justified this by saying, "Yet I cannot believe that, just because one has a wife and children, he is free to offend God by lying (not to mention all the other things he would be called upon to do)."[52]

The high point of his resistance came with his refusal to accept military service. The reasons for refusal were two: The war was unjust and service in the army would constitute an occasion of sin for him.[53] Arguments against this stand were presented by his pastor and other priests, by neighbors, and members of his family—but to no avail. The arguments Jaegerstaetter used centered around the necessity of the individual making a private judgment on what things really belonged to Caesar and what belonged to God and on the necessity of the dictates of conscience taking precedence even over such personal considerations as family responsibilities.[54] Jaegerstaetter persisted in this stand, even refusing a guarantee of noncombatant service offered by the military tribunal, because the Nazi regime persecuted his Church and the war was unjust. In a statement written immediately before his death, he made his position clear: "You will not find it written in any of the commandments of God or of the Church that a man is obliged under pain of sin to take an oath committing him to obey whatever might be commanded of him by his secular ruler."[55] For his act of political opposition, which was deeply rooted in religious convictions, Jaegerstaetter was beheaded on 9 August 1943.

A more influential voice of protest against the Nazi regime was that of Clement von Galen, the Bishop of Muenster. This distinguished churchman is best known for his condemnation of the euthanasia program, introduced by the Third Reich on 1 September 1939 and intended to apply to all persons with incurable diseases, either mental or physical. The method of

---

[52] *Ibid.*, p. 53.

[53] *Ibid.*, p. 57.

[54] *Ibid.*, p. 87.

[55] *Ibid.*, pp. 101-102.

extermination at first was shooting; later gas was used with cremation following.[56]

Though the project was classified top secret, its existence gradually became known. In August, 1940, Cardinal Bertram protested to the Government that this policy seriously contradicted Catholic moral law, in addition to offending the moral sense of the German people. This protest was coupled with a sermon preached by von Galen on 3 August 1941 in Muenster in which he gave a detailed report on the euthanasia program and condemned it in very severe terms. Reports of the sermon spread across Germany rapidly and "this protest struck such a responsive chord and increased his popularity so enormously that the government found it impossible to proceed against him."[57]

Although some Nazi officials wanted to have von Galen taken into custody, his protest and the support it received from the people led to a termination of the program shortly after the sermon. From time to time, the German bishops would reiterate in sermons or pastoral letters continued opposition to such programs, which possibly helped in halting a re-introduction of the euthanasia program. Indeed, Lewy considers this reaction of the Catholic Church as being the major force in effecting the termination of this program.[58] Public protest helped form and solidify public opinion which, in turn, led to the termination of the program.

In different ways, both cases present specific examples in which obedience to the State was exercised selectively. In Jaegerstaetter's case it was more a matter of rejecting a regime which he regarded as immoral; though he did not "revolt" in the usual sense, he avoided voluntary cooperation whenever possible. His reason for this is as follows.

I can easily see that anyone who refuses to acknowledge the Nazi Folk Community and also is unwilling to comply with all the demands of its leaders will thereby forfeit the rights and

---

[56] Lewy, *The Catholic Church and Nazi Germany, op. cit.*, p. 263.

[57] *Ibid.*, p. 265.

[58] *Ibid.*, p. 266.

privileges offered by that nation. But it is not much different with God. He who does not wish to acknowledge the community of saints or who does not obey all the commandments set forth by Him and His Church and who is not ready to undergo sacrifices and to fight for His Kingdom either—such a one also loses every claim and every right under that Kingdom. . . . Now anyone who is able to fight for both kingdoms and stay in good standing in both communities (that is, the community of saints and the Nazi Folk Community) and who is able to obey every command of the Third Reich—such a man, in my opinion would have to be a great magician. I for one cannot do so.[59]

Bishop von Galen, while he also disapproved of Hitler and his Government, limited his open opposition to specific programs and activities of the Third Reich. (It is interesting to note that even in his strongest denunciations, the bishop called for loyal service by Catholics in supporting the war effort.)

Few, if any, would challenge that unjust wars and euthanasia constitute areas in which obedience could not be given because of conflicts with Catholic moral teaching; both are clear violations of the Fifth Commandment, however generously one might wish to interpret that most basic norm of morality. Those who would reject the principle of selective obedience and would speak instead of the presumption of justice must come to terms with cases such as these. Either Jaegerstaetter, von Galen and all the others were right and deserve the honor they have received, or they must be charged with acting with an "erroneous conscience" by refusing the obedience owed to the State.

If such examples are treated as exceptions, there are many other areas which present similar problems: racism expressed in Jim Crow legislation, the use of torture, and the repression or distortion of information in the media, etc. The theory of selective obedience faces up to these problems and recognizes the limitations of the presumption of justice principle. It holds that the actions of a Government may not be presumed to be

---

[59] Gordon Zahn, *In Solitary Witness* (Boston: Beacon Press, 1968), p. 205.

either just or unjust; rather, they must be subjected to critical examination in the light of religious and political values and judgment pronounced, whether on an individual or institutional basis, on their conformity or non-conformity to primary and ultimate values. Obedience or disobedience will follow this critical examination and will be, therefore, a deliberate moral act. If one wishes to argue against the theory of selective obedience to the State in such instances, a more compelling case for the presumption of justice must be made than Rohr and others have been able to present. A Jaegerstaetter rejecting military service in a war he recognized as unjust—or the millions of his fellow Catholics who either failed to question the morality of the war or quieted whatever doubts they may have had and "did their duty" believing they could do nothing else: one must choose between them. To choose Jaegerstaetter as the better model of Christian behavior is to choose the principle of selective obedience over the uncritical presumption of justice principle as the measure of responsible moral action.

E. Summary Statement

This chapter has examined the theory of selective obedience from the perspective of public policy. The basic arguments raised against selective obedience were stated in terms of the presumed justice of the Government's cause, the threat of anarchy, and compelling Government interests. However, as the chapter shows, most of the arguments used to support these claims either from hypothetical premises or, as in the court decisions cited, do no more than assert a compelling Government interest without stating these interests.

What these case studies have indicated, however, are continuing areas of tension between either the individual and Government or an institutional religion and Government. The theory of selective obedience is not presented as a resolution of these tensions but rather to affirm a principle to be used in resolving these tensions. The principle is the qualification of political obligation because of compelling religious interests or values. And while this principle does not in itself determine when to obey or disobey or which political obligations to question, it does demand the necessity of maintaining fidelity to the more significant religious values, even while engaged in the political processes.

The problem of the right of the majority and the evaluation of claims to limit obedience in the name of higher loyalty will always be areas a theory of selective obedience will have to consider and determine. This theory necessarily focuses attention on the rights of the minority as well as on claims to a higher loyalty. The effective application of a theory of selective obedience must extend in principle to as wide a range of issues as possible to ensure inclusion of all relevant values and interests. In this way the threat of irresponsibility in selective obedience will be minimized through continued insistence that responsibility to the larger community, as well as responsibility to religious commitments, must be taken into account. Thus it is not enough simply to make the *claim* that the policy is unjust or that the particular group should be exempted from it. An actual case, demonstrating real and serious harm to religious values, the discriminatory nature of the policy of the State and the damage incurred by the group in question must be demonstrated. The claim for selectivity must be justified and the policy of the State shown to be contradictory to the values in question. This will be accomplished by testing the claim in terms of both religious values and public policy for the case for selectivity in obedience to be established.[60] In this way, the rights of both the majority and the minority are protected for selectivity in obedience must go beyond the claim of an exemption from a policy to the establishment of an argument, tested by religious values and public policy, which is convincing.

It should also be noted that the theory of selective obedience will generally come into effect in crisis situations or in a period of time when values or loyalties are challenged. The

---

[60] This does not imply that the State will recognize this claim; this possibility implies a continued tension between the loyalties owed to Church and State.

Vietnam war, for example, raised such value questions in the last decade and it is possible that the legalization of abortion will pose similar value problems in the years to come. As such, selective obedience presents itself as a relevant moral position for times of crisis.

Chapter VII
Conclusion

A. General Conclusions

The dominant theory of the Roman Catholic tradition of Church-Government relations, especially after the Counter-Reformation has been to favor the obedience of the individual Catholic and the institution of the Church to the State. This has been challenged by the theory and practice of disobedience to the State, but this has always remained within a subordinate position within the Church's tradition. The basic felt tradition has favored assuming the duty of the Catholic and the Church to obey secular authority because it indirectly reflects the authority of God. This reasoning is based on a hierarchically ordered universe in which the supernatural order is understood as the fulfillment and transcendent norm for ordering the natural sphere. This teaching is also supported through reference to the New Testament, which is used as the foundation for the two-sword theory and the separation of civic from religious responsibilities. One may argue with the adequacy of the Thomistic model and the philosophical foundation on which it rests, as well as realizing that it is possible to defend a variety of Church-State relations on the basis of either the different traditions within the New Testament or a selective reading of some of the texts. Still the Catholic is faced with the tradition and practice of obedience easily being given to the State, as well as the accommodation of the Church to society with the consequent surrender of power. Thus the problem of this book has been to re-examine elements of this tradition to investigate the possibility of establishing a theory of selective obedience to the State.

Within the tradition, there has always been the principle that God is to be obeyed rather than man. The tradition has dealt with this by suspending it, that is, by regarding it as an extreme principle to be used only in rarely occurring situations, or by hedging it about with a maze of qualifications so that its strength was greatly diminished. However, the principle of obedience to God serves as a residual element of the prophetic dimension of the Catholic Church in that it proclaims the priority that should be given to religious values. Although the prophetic element is not a significant quality of the church type, this principle functions within the Church as a reminder, however weak and limited, of the priorities that the Church should seek in arranging its relations with secular institutions.

Together with this principle, there are two other elements within recent official Catholic teaching which promise a redirection of emphasis in Church-Government relations. The first of these is given in *Pacem in Terris:* "Those therefore who have authority in the state may oblige men in conscience only if their authority is intrinsically related with the authority of God and shares in it" (no. 49). The second is found in *Dignitas Humanae* of Vatican II: ". . . all men are to be immune from coercion in such wise that in matters religious no one is to be forced to act in a manner contrary to his own beliefs" (no. 2). This statement also indicates that no one, within due limits, is to be restrained from acting in accordance with his or her religious beliefs. Both of these principles were anticipated in Zahn's analysis of the role of the Church in society. After tracing the accommodation of the Church to the values of secular society and its role in supplementing the social controls of the secular order, Zahn proposes instead a positive program which calls for a detachment of the Church from secular and nationalistic interests, an emphasis on fortitude rather than prudence, a reawakening of the ascetic ideal of the early Church, and a reaffirmation of the ability of and the necessity for the individual to make responsible moral decisions. This formulation, together with the insistence that the Church be certain that obedience is called for before it obeys or counsels others to obey, sharpens the thrust of recent official teaching. The emphasis would now be placed upon the priority of religious values and in this shift of emphasis we find the justification for a theory of selective obedience to the State.

These principles can be incorporated into a description of the Church and its role in society to form the framework for a theory of selective obedience. Such a description of the Church focuses on five elements. The first is the necessity for the Church to act at times as a sect because of severe threats to values that it perceives as crucial to its own self-understanding and hierarchy of values. The Church, therefore, is not to assume *a priori* any fixed relation between it and the Government other than that of a continuing evaluation of policies and values proposed by the Government. The second is the necessity of the Church's retaining fidelity to its essential values even though they may not be in full accord with the definition of these values as proposed by the larger society. Through revelation, tradition and the natural law, the Church maintains a transcendent point of reference in defining values and this constitutes the foundation of the selective behavior of the Church and its members in society. The third is the common good, used as a progressive principle to ensure that the benefits of society, especially in terms of employment, political equality and social justice, are not limited to a select few. Such a specification of justice would impose a limitation upon support to specific programs or policies of the State under which significant numbers of the citizens do or could suffer injustice. The fourth is the primacy of the values of the Church even though it is a secondary association by virtue of exclusiveness of membership. This indicates that the behavior in a primary institution such as the State can be qualified by the values of a secondary association. The final element is the eschatological nature of the Church which implies that the fulfillment of the Church comes only from the future—the Kingdom—and that its present institutional existence is an incomplete articulation of its full meaning and life. This requires that the Church stand in a relation of critical negativity to itself and the societies with which it interacts because it knows that there is a continual need for a greater actualization of the Church's values.

Though a member of the Church, the Catholic is still a citizen and the Church still exists within the larger institution of the State. As such, both incur political obligations. The natural authority of the State, the acceptance of benefits of the State, the obedience owed just institutions, and the mutuality between citizens in terms of cooperative restriction of behavior all constitute *prima facie* obligations to the Government which cannot be dismissed lightly. These obligations may be strengthened, qualified or terminated, however, under the concept of the pluralist citizen, one who shares in ruling and being ruled through membership in different associations, taken together with the religious values of the Church and its relation to society, as described above. The concept of the pluralist citizen, as defined by Walzer, rests upon the fact of competing claims occurring between Government and voluntary or secondary associations to which the individual belongs. This forms the basic secular and political framework in which the citizen exists. The religious values of the Catholic Church and its relation to the State form the content of this framework by specifying the normative values to be used by the Catholic citizen in judging between competing claims and evaluating his or her political obligations. Political obligations are taken seriously by the Catholic citizen, but they must always be judged in the light of transcendent values. Because of this obligation of continued evaluation of the policies, strategies, and values of the nation-state, the obedience of the Catholic citizen must always of necessity be selective; for in no instance can the Catholic citizen automatically presume a necessary harmony of values between Church and Government. Nor may the Catholic citizen surrender his or her duty to judge the State's values or policies in the light of religious values and obligations.

The use of several elements of contemporary contractual theory to help establish more clearly the sources of political obligation serves, in this book, as a corrective to traditional Roman Catholic organic social theory. This is necessary to help specify the political obligations of the Catholic citizen within a democratic society. Therefore, the organic theory of society is not challenged as such. The book incorporates some elements of contemporary contractual theory into the organic model as a means of clarifying and specifying political obligations not easily handled by traditional organic theory.

The opening for this comes from the writings of John Courtney Murray, who reworked Roman Catholic social philosophy in terms of American democratic society, and from the documents of Vatican II and their restatement of the Church-Government problem. Both of these sources respect the proper autonomy of the State and its right to make independent political, moral decisions which are binding on citizens as well as indicating that one of the State's proper tasks is the promotion of the dignity of the human person by allowing the person to enjoy rights and to fulfill duties. This establishes a much more active role for the citizen than organic theory envisions, although in the classic Thomistic model, the mode in which the indirect divine authority of the State was to be exercised was seen as coming indirectly through the citizens. This is more fully developed by Rommen in his analysis of the translation model of the origin of political authority. This model states that although all authority ultimately rests wtih God, political authority resides within the community organized as the body politic and is vested by it in the ruler. Thus, there are clear implications of contractualism within the classic organic model which this book further specifies through the use of contemporary contractual analysis. The more active role of the citizen in civil affairs and the shared responsibility in ruling through participation in public policy make it necessary to specify more clearly the sources of political obligation. This has been accomplished with the categories provided by Walzer, Childress, Rawls, and Sibley, as described above. What these categories do is specify the general obligations of citizenship provided by the organic model in a way that makes the organic model more functional in a democratic society. Using the organic model as a basis allows the retention of the natural unity of society and its members while the addition of the contractual elements helps specify the obligations of the citizens to each other, to the State and to other secondary associations to which they may belong. In this way, the defect of extreme individualism which a radical contractual model could promote is avoided and the unity of the society is preserved through the retention of the organic model, while avoiding the danger of too narrow or static an understanding of the role of the citizen.

B. Emerging Issues

In the development of the argument of this book, several issues emerged which were clearly related to its problem but which could not be resolved without departing somewhat from the more sharply defined focus of the book. This section will touch upon some of these issues, if only to show their relation to the central problem of the book and to indicate other areas of possible application of the theory of selective obedience.

The theory of selective obedience has been treated here from the perspective and tradition of Roman Catholicism and the case has been made for its being an important part of Roman Catholic social philosophy. This should not be understood as restricting its application to this particular religious community and its membership. Rather, it can be argued that this is a universal principle, especially in the light of Walzer's category of the pluralist citizen which states that competing claims from other associations may significantly qualify the *prima facie* obligation of the citizen to obey the State. This, in turn, is rooted in willfulness of membership in the State and emerging consent to its policies. Both considerations could support the framework of a general theory of selective obedience within democratic societies. What must be thoroughly established is the basis upon which claims to selectivity in obedience are to be made in terms of public policy. In this instance, careful and convincing arguments must be presented so that the rights of the minority *and* the majority are protected. In this model, no claim may be acted upon unless arguments are presented, consequences are calculated, the effect on the common good evaluated, and the principle of proportionality observed. The methodology seeks a clarification of policy and the protection of the rights of all concerned as well as establishing the claim for preferential treatment. The argument suggests the potential universality of the theory of selective obedience, but does not attempt a thorough justification of the principle nor does it provide the methodology for establishing such claims. However, the establishment and discussion of this principle within Roman Catholic social philosophy does indicate aspects of the theory that could be generalized, such as the qualification of *prima facie* ordering of competing claims and obligations, as well as some elements that must be taken into account in justifying such a claim for selectivity, such as the requirements of the common good and the principle of proportionality.

Another element in this book that deserves elaboration is the prophetic tradition within Roman Catholicism. Although the subject of prophecy has been a popular one in recent years and many actions, especially anti-war actions, have been described as prophetic, few serious works on a theology of prophecy have appeared. Yet the prophetic (or charismatic or sectarian) element has been an important aspect of Catholicism. The rise and growth of the major religious orders, for example, has always been understood as a prophetic element which served as a means of reform within both Church and the larger society. Pius XII indicated the presence and value of prophecy within the Church in his encyclical *Mystici Corporis (The Mystical Body)* by teaching that Christ can single out from the Church, especially in grave times, persons of conspicuous holiness to point the way to perfection.

The value of this prophetic dimension of Catholicism has been analyzed and developed by Zahn whose writings have formed a partial basis for elements of this book. This has emphasized the sociological aspects of prophecy in developing a theory of selective obedience by analyzing the necessity of elements within the Church acting in a sectarian manner to effect reform in both Church and State. But there is a two-way relationship here. Just as selective obedience can be seen as a reflection of or a vehicle for prophecy, the theory of selective obedience could open the way to the restoration of prophecy to a more fully honored and accepted place within the Church and its social philosophy. Such renewed recognition of prophecy as a vital religious force within the Church would help the Church and its members become more aware of crucial social problems and would help the process of reform by ensuring that issues that needed to be discussed are not submerged within the bureaucracy of the institution. This is not to argue that the institutional dimension of the Church should be destroyed or viewed as utterly useless. Rather it is a suggestion that the totality of the Church consists of many realities and prophecy is one essential mechanism by which its mission is to be served and ultimately fulfilled. This book can do little more than note the importance of the prophetic principle within Catholicism, but it recognizes that a more thorough analysis is needed. Hopefully the acceptance of the theory of selective obedience will provide motivation for further exploration.

On quite another level we find the issue of amnesty which is increasingly the source of political controversy in the United States. In a sense, selective obedience could be construed as a type of "after the fact" recognition of one of the applications of this principle. Many of those who refused to serve in the Armed Forces and who actually deserted from military service did so because of conscientious objection to a particular war or a particular policy of the Government in pursuing the war. While not proposing this to be a blanket justification for all who refused service in the Vietnam war, there is no doubt that many such refusals represented selective conscientious objection to the war and this takes on a special significance in the case of members of the Roman Catholic Church. The acceptance in Catholic social philosophy of the theory of selective obedience to the State could provide additional evidence for the justification of such refusal when the sincerity of their objections is established. The theory would provide *post factum* justification for refusal to cooperate with an unjust policy of the State. This interpretation—and, by implication, the theory itself—finds some support in the official position taken by the United States Catholic Conference in support of amnesty.

In the Supreme Court case *Roe v. Wade* (22 January 1973) we find another issue which has significant implications for Church-Government relations. Basically the Court decided in *Roe v. Wade* that the Texas statutes on abortion improperly violated the right of a woman to terminate her pregnancy. The Court's main argument was that the right of privacy, which was grounded in the 14th Amendment's concept of personal liberty and restrictions upon State action and the Ninth Amendment's reservation of rights to the people, was broad enough to encompass a woman's desire to terminate or not to terminate her pregnancy. The Court also noted that past abortion laws were the result of a combination of factors: Victorian social concern which discouraged illicit sexual conduct, abortion's being a hazardous medical procedure, and the State's interest in protecting prenatal life. In another state of the argument, the Court argued that "person" as used in the 14th Amendment did not include the unborn and that the unborn have never been recognized in law as persons in the whole sense. The Court also noted that the State has an interest in the health of the pregnant woman; this interest becomes compelling after the first trimester because of a higher maternal mortality rate for abortions performed after this time. The State also has an interest in the potentiality of human life; this interest becomes compelling after viability, for which reason abortion is then to be proscribed unless it is necessary for the health of the mother.

The major conclusion that the Court drew from its line of reasoning was that the State criminal abortion statutes which exempt from criminality only a lifesaving procedure in behalf of the mother without regard to pregnancy states and without recognition of other interests involved are in violation of the Due Process Clause of the 14th Amendment. This conclusion has three implications: (1) prior to the end of the first trimester, an abortion decision is to be left to the medical judgment of the woman's doctor; (2) after the first trimester, the State, in promoting the health of the mother, may regulate the abortion procedure in ways reasonably related to maternal health; (3) for the stage subsequent to viability the State, in promoting its interest in the potentiality of human life, may regulate and proscribe abortions except when necessary in appropriate medical judgment, for the preservation of the life and health of the mother. As a consequence of this decision, the vast majority of abortion statutes in the United States have been rendered inoperative. Yet it is important to remember that this decision does not force or require any woman to have an abortion; it states that the woman, at least in the first trimester, may not be restrained from obtaining an abortion.

As it stands, what is now permitted by the Supreme Court is in total contradiction to the teaching and practice of the Roman Catholic Church.[1] On one level, however, the abortion decision of the Court will not have a direct effect on Catholic women who are pregnant for they will not be required to obtain an abortion and if they are faithful to the teaching of the Church, they will not seek one. On another level, of considerable interest to the topic of this book, the abortion decision can affect Catholic hospitals, doctors and nurses for they may be required to participate in abortion procedures, an action which is also forbidden by the Church. In addition, the use of public funds to support either abortion clinics or abortion procedures needs to be evaluated by Catholics. For if such funds were taken from tax monies, as is likely to be the case, it would very likely be an immoral form of cooperation in evil for a Catholic to pay that portion of taxes which would be used for this purpose. As such these possible situations present a conflict between Church and Government and provide another example of the applicability of selective obedience to the State.

An editorial in *Commonweal* reports several problems relative to hospitals and their staffs.[2] A bill in the Oregon Legislature would require Catholic hospitals to admit patients for

---

[1] Abortion is defined as the "deliberate ejection from the womb of an unviable fetus." All those who effectively procure an abortion, including the mother, are excommunicated (canon 2350). As such, this definition does not include an operation or the taking of medicine to preserve the health of the mother which may produce, as an unintended and involuntary consequence, an abortion. This is based upon the principle of the double effect. Consult Marcian Mathis, O.F.M. and Dismas Bonner, O.F.M., *The Pastoral Companion* (Chicago: Franciscan Herald Press, 1967, 13th edition), p. 133.

[2] "Abortion: Next Round," *Commonweal* 98 (23 March 1973), p. 51.

abortion procedures; Wisconsin has a measure threatening the licenses of doctors and nurses who refuse to perform an abortion; a Federal district court in Montana compelled a Catholic hospital to allow its facilities to be used for a sterilization operation, not an abortion procedure obviously, but an action forbidden by traditional Catholic morality.

The ground upon which these proceedings are based is the reception of public funds by Catholic hospitals under the Hill-Burton Act. This Act, originally passed in 1946 and amended many times since, provided for the expansion of hospital services. Section 622 of the Act provides that hospitals will be available to all persons regardless of race, creed or color, or financial condition. Since many Catholic hospitals have been the recipient of such funds, they are particularly vulnerable to Government disposition and mandate. The same *Commonweal* editorial states the issue quite clearly.

Equally large numbers of these hospitals have received funds for research and other projects under government sponsored National Institute of Health programs, a detail which could increase the legal jeopardy of these institutions should a precedent be established whereby courts or legislatures made receipt of public funds a determinant in which public services or a medical institution performed. Hospitals that received Hill-Burton funds would seem to be particularly vulnerable, since these funds are extended on conditions which, surprisingly, need not be presented by the government prior to acceptance of the grant or loan.[3]

Such a determination of hospital or health facility policy by Government presents a serious challenge to the Church, as well as raising questions of religious freedom and civil rights.

The official Catholic reaction to this situation has been rapid and firm. Catholic bishops and large numbers of Catholic laity have voiced very strong opposition to the Court's decision and to the concept of abortion on demand. Bishops have supported and encouraged the formation of right to life groups which would attempt to create a pro-life mentality and to oppose the Court's decision and laws reflecting its orientation.

[3] *Ibid.,* p. 51.

In discussing the Court's decision, American Catholic bishops used some unusually strong language to voice their opposition. Two quotations from their statement provide evidence of this.

This opinion of the Court fails to protect the most basic human right—the right to life. Therefore, we reject this decision of the Court because, as John XXIII says, "If any government does not acknowledge the rights of man or violates them, . . . its orders completely lack juridical force."[4]

Thus, the laws that conform to the opinion of the Court are immoral laws, in opposition to God's plan of creation and to the Divine Law which prohibits the destruction of human life at any point of its existence. Whenever a conflict arises between the law of God and any human laws, we are held to follow God's law.[5]

One pastoral application the bishops draw from these principles is that "Catholics must oppose abortion as an immoral act. No one is obliged to obey any civil law that may require abortion."[6] Another is pursuing protection for institutions or individuals who refuse on the basis of conscience to engage in abortion procedures. One other application, suggested by Cardinal Cody of Chicago, is that Catholics may have an obligation to protest the use of tax monies for abortion purposes.[7] While this proposal does not actually demand the refusal of payment of taxes or a portion of them, it is an extremely radical statement from an American Catholic Cardinal and is indicative of the seriousness of the official Catholic opposition to abortion.

These official statements of the hierarchy suggest that a very serious conflict between Church and State is in the making. For if Catholics in hospitals or clinics are forced by law to participate in actions repugnant to both their conscience and

---

[4] Pastoral Message of the Administrative Committee. National Conference of Catholic Bishops, 13 February 1973 (Washington, D.C.: United States Catholic Conference).

[5] *Ibid.*

[6] *Ibid.*

[7] Rick Casey, "Bishops Condemn Abortion Decision," *National Catholic Reporter* (23 February 1973), p. 2.

Church teaching, serious harm will be done to religious and civil liberties, together with possible job discrimination because of religious preference. Some states are proposing legislation to protect the conscientious rights of persons in this area. An example of this is S. 1568, introduced to the Massachusetts Legislature by Kevin Harrington. This bill basically states that no hospital shall be required to admit any patient for the purpose of obtaining an abortion, a sterilization procedure or contraceptive devices or information. Doctors, nurses and staff who conscientiously object to these procedures will not be required to perform them.

There is, as was noted above, legislation seeking the exact opposite and legislation such as the Massachusetts bill has yet to be tested in relation to both the Supreme Court decision and the provisions of the Hill-Burton Act. There is also a great deal of public pressure against legislation such as that proposed by Harrington. As a result, confusion exists and procedures and policies of both hospitals and the law are unclear. Yet, the practice called for on the part of Catholics is clear. But the protection of such conscientious action is not yet protected by legislation or juridical procedures.

The hierarchy and Catholics who follow its teaching may find themselves in the position of refusing to obey certain laws or of refusing to participate in certain procedures at the risk of fines or loss of employment. As long as abortions are merely "permitted," this may not be the case; but if hospitals are required to provide such procedures and the staff required to perform them, regardless of conscientious objections, then Catholics have no choice but to disobey the law if they wish to remain faithful to the Church's teaching and their conscience.

This type of situation provides another example of the applicability of the theory of selective obedience to the State. The hierarchy has not argued that the Government as a whole is immoral or not deserving of allegiance. Nor has there been a call for total civil disobedience or for a removal of the Government or of certain legislators. Rather the bishops have argued that certain laws and policies are not in conformity with God's law and therefore these laws should not be obeyed;

all other laws which pass this test are in force and are to be obeyed. The bishops are claiming the right to pick and choose which laws they wish to obey and are doing this on the basis of religious motivation. In effect, they are claiming the right and duty to selectively obey the laws of the land. The bishops present no general arguments for this selectivity nor do they propose a theory of selective obedience as such. Yet two arguments used by the bishops—the supremacy of divine over human laws and the lack of juridical force of orders which violate the rights of the person—are two of the general arguments used to support a general theory of selective obedience in this book. And the other arguments proposed here can give theological and political support to the position called for by the bishops. Thus, the general theory of selective obedience takes on a greater importance in this crucial discussion of civil and religious rights because it can provide an ethical-political principle which will help determine and justify such selectivity in the practice of Catholics who may be required to participate in abortion procedures.

This discussion deals with a potential legal conflict between Church and State and as such is hypothetical. Yet it is an important discussion because such a conflict may really arise in the near future. The Catholic bishops have already demanded selectivity in obedience but have not provided a total rationale for such a practice. Also it will be most important for the Church to have as coherent an argument as possible to justify its selective behavior for the courts. And it will be important for the Church to demonstrate that such selectivity is not simply an emotional or ideological reaction supported only by anti-abortion propaganda, but rather is an ethical principle derived from the Church's social philosophy.

If the Church is to provide real leadership and facilitate a rational discussion of the issues involved, it must present a coherent theory justifying its position, especially if the Church's anti-abortion position would imply disobedience to some federal and/or state laws. The general theory of selective obedience proposed here can be one element of this discussion for it provides justification for selectivity in obedience based on an analysis of Catholic social philosophy, dogma and political obligation. As such, this can be an important element in justifying the practice of Catholics who may be required by the hierarchy or their consciences to disobey certain laws while not denying their general political obligations to the State or to their fellow citizens. The theory of selective obedience can provide Catholics with a tool to clarify their present position and to develop principles and strategies in advance so that the Church will not be in the position of simply reacting to situations as they occur.

The explosive potential of this principle of selective obedience has been noted. Nevertheless, arguments raised against this principle in the concrete cases cited either have been hypothetical, or have not clearly indicated the compelling Government interests that would be endangered and, to some degree, have indicated a discrimination against a religion such as Roman Catholicism which incorporates selectivity in its position vis-à-vis the Government. The fear of anarchy, advanced as another argument against selective obedience, would make sense only in situations where there is a total lack of justice in the policies of the State as well as an absence of means of reform. Selective obedience is not anarchy; it is, instead, a prudent awareness that in particular areas a governmental policy may be unjust and obedience should be refused. It must always be remembered that the theory of selective obedience is a theory of obedience; the extent to which obedience is or is not forthcoming is determined by the extent to which the State does or does not serve the common good.

Because of the very nature of Church and Government, competing claims and areas of tension between them have occurred and are certain to recur throughout history. The principle of selective obedience, rooted in the oldest traditions of the Church as well as recent official Church teaching, does not offer a methodology for resolving these tensions. Rather it provides an ethical principle, rooted in religious values and political theory, which must be used as a point of departure in evaluating the claims of the State on the Catholic citizen. This ethical principle states that the claims of the nation-state must be evaluated in the light of their compatibility with the transcendent norms of the Church before obedience can be given. The principle of selective obedience does not, therefore, determine an *a priori* position of the Church vis-à-vis the State; it merely suggests that an evaluation of State policy must be conducted before obedience can be given—or withheld.

Bibliography

Books

Abbott, Walter M., S.J., Ed. *The Documents of Vatican II*. New York: Guild Press, 1966.

Abell, Aaron I. *American Catholicism and Social Action, 1865-1950*. Garden City, New York: Hanover House, 1960.

Addison, James T. *War, Peace and the Christian Mind.* Greenwich, Conn.: Seabury Press, 1963.

Arendt, Hannah, *Crises of the Republic*. New York: Harcourt Brace Jovanovich, Inc., 1972.

Baierl, Joseph J. *The Catholic Church and the Modern State*. Rochester, New York: St. Bernard's Seminary, 1955.

Bainton, Roland H. *Christian Attitudes Toward War and Peace*. New York: Abingdon Press, 1960.

———. *Early Christianity*. Princeton, New Jersey: D. Van Nostrand Co., Inc., 1960.

Bennett, John C. *Christian Ethics and Social Policy*. New York: Charles Scribner's Sons, 1946.

———. *Christians and the State*. New York: Charles Scribner's Sons, 1962.

———. *Nuclear Weapons and the Conflict of Conscience*. New York: Charles Scribner's Sons, 1962.

Bier, William C., S.J., Ed. *Conscience: Its Freedom and Limitation*. New York: Fordham University Press, 1971.

Boeckle, Franz. *Fundamental Concepts of Moral Theology*. Trans. by William Jerman. New York: Paulist Press, 1968.

Bowe, Gabriel. *The Origin of Political Authority*. Dublin: Clonmore and Reynolds, 1955.

Browne-Lof, Lillian. *Pius XI: Apostle of Peace*. New York: The Macmillan Company, 1938.

Bruehl, Charles P. *The Pope's Plan for Social Reconstruction*. New York: The Devin-Adair Co., 1939.

Caird, G. B. *The Apostolic Age*. London: Gerald Duckworth and Co., Ltd., 1966.

Calves, J. Y., S.J. *The Social Thought of John XXIII*. Trans. by George W. McKenzie, S.M. Chicago: Henry Regnery Co., 1964.

Camp, Richard L. *The Papal Ideology of Social Reform*. Leiden: E. J. Brill, 1969.

Carlyle, Sir R. W. and A. J. Carlyle. *A History of Mediaeval Politi-*

cal Theory in the West. Vols. I-V. New York: Barnes and Noble, Inc., 4th printing, no date.

Childress, James F. *Civil Disobedience and Political Obligation.* New Haven: Yale University Press, 1971.

Chinigo, Michael, Ed. *The Pope Speaks.* New York: Pantheon Books, Inc., 1957.

————. *The Teachings of Pope Pius XII.* London: Methuen and Co., Ltd., 1958.

Cianfarra, Camille. *The Vatican and the War.* New York: E. P. Dutton and Co., Inc., 1945.

Croner, John F. *The Catholic as Citizen.* Baltimore: Helicon Press, 1963.

Cullmann, Oscar. *Jesus and the Revolutionaries.* Trans. by Gareth Putnam. New York: Harper and Row, 1970.

————. *The State in the New Testament.* London: SCM Press, Ltd., 1957.

D'Arcy, Eric. *Conscience and Its Right to Freedom.* New York: Sheed and Ward, 1960.

Davis, Thurston N., Ed. *Between Two Cities.* Chicago: Loyola University Press, 1962.

Dawson, Christopher. *Religion and the Modern State.* London: Sheed and Ward, 1935.

————. *Beyond Politics.* New York: Sheed and Ward, 1939.

Deane, Herbert A. *The Political Ideas of Harold J. Laski.* New York: Columbia University Press, 1955.

————. *The Political and Social Ideas of St. Augustine.* New York: Columbia University Press, 1963.

Delhaye, Phillipe. *The Christian Conscience.* Trans. by Charles U. Quinn. New York: Desclee Co., 1968.

Dohen, Dorothy, *Nationalism and American Catholicism.* New York: Sheed and Ward, 1967.

Douglas, James W. *The Non-Violent Cross.* London: Collier-Macmillan, Ltd., 1966.

Drinan, Robert F., S.J. *Religion, the Courts and Public Policy.* New York: McGraw-Hill, 1963.

Ehler, Sidney Z. and John B. Morrall, Eds. *Church and State Through the Centuries.* London: Burns and Oates, 1954.

Emanuel, Cyprian, O.F.M., Ed. *The Morality of Conscientious Objection to War.* Washington, D.C.: Catholic Association for International Peace, 1942.

Finn, James, Ed. *A Conflict of Loyalties.* New York: Pegasus, 1968.

Fremantle, Anne, Ed. *The Social Teaching of the Church.* New York: Mentor-Omega Book, 1963.

Friedlaender, Saul. *Pius XII and the Third Reich.* Trans. by Charles Fullman. New York: Alfred A. Knopf, 1966.

Genicot, E., S.J. *Institutiones Theologiae Morales.* Vols. 1 and 2. Bruges: Desclee De Brouwer, 17th ed., 1959.

Giannella, Donald, Ed. *Religion and the Public Order.* Vol. 4. Ithaca: Cornell University Press, 1968.

Gibbons, William J., S.J., Ed. *Seven Great Encyclicals.* Glen Rock, New Jersey: Paulist Press, 1963.

Gilby, Thomas, Ed. *St. Thomas Aquinas: Philosophical Texts.* New York: Oxford University Press, 1960.

Graham, Robert A., S.J. *Vatican Diplomacy: A Study of Church and State on the International Plane.* Princeton: Princeton University Press, 1959.

Hales, E. E. Y. *The Catholic Church in the Modern World.* Garden City, New York: Image Books, 1960.

———. *Pio Nono: A Study in European Politics and Religion in the Nineteenth Century.* New York: P. J. Kenedy and Sons, 1954.

Haering, Bernard, C.SS.R. *The Law of Christ.* Vols. 1-3. Trans. by Edwin Kaiser, C.PP.S. Westminster, Maryland: The Newman Press, 1966.

———. *A Theology of Protest.* New York: Farrar, Straus and Geroux, 1970.

Husslein, Joseph, Ed. *Social Wellsprings.* Vol. I. Milwaukee: The Bruce Publishing Co., 1940.

Jaszi, Oscar and John D. Lewis. *Against the Tyrant.* Glencoe, Ill.: The Free Press, 1957.

Kerwin, Jerome G. *Catholic Viewpoint on Church and State.* Garden City, New York: Hanover House, 1960.

———. *Politics, Government, Catholics.* New York: Paulist Press, 1961.

Laski, Harold J. *A Grammar of Politics.* New Haven: Yale University Press, 1925.

———. *Studies in the Problem of Sovereignty.* New Haven: Yale University Press, 1937.

———. *Authority in the Modern State.* New Haven: Yale University Press, 1927.

———. *Liberty in the Modern State.* New York: Viking Press, 1949.

———. *Democracy in Crisis.* The University of North Carolina Press, 1935.

———. *An Introduction to Politics.* London: George Allen and Univen, Ltd., 1951.

———. *The State in Theory and Practice.* New York: The Viking Press, 1935.

———. *The American Democracy.* New York: The Viking Press, 1948.

Lee, Robert, Ed. *Religion and Social Conflict*. New York: Oxford University Press, 1964.

Lewy, Guenter. *The Catholic Church and Nazi Germany*. New York: McGraw-Hill, 1964.

Love, Thomas T. *John Courtney Murray: Contemporary Church-State Theory*. Garden City, New York: Doubleday and Co., Inc., 1965.

McLaughlin, Terrence, C.S.B., Ed. *The Church and the Reconstruction of the Modern World: The Social Encyclicals of Pope Pius XI*. Garden City, New York: Image Books, 1957.

Maritain, Jacques. *Christianity and Democracy*. Trans. by Doris C. Anson. New York: Charles Scribner's Sons, 1944.

———. *Integral Humanism*. Trans. by Joseph W. Evans. New York: Charles Scribner's Sons, 1968.

———. *Man and the State*. Chicago: University of Chicago Press, 1951.

———. *The Person and the Common Good*. Trans. by John J. Fitzgerald. New York: Charles Scribner's Sons, 1947.

———. *The Rights of Man and Natural Law*. London: The Centenary Press, 1944.

———. *The Things That Are Not Caesar's*. Trans. by J. F. Scanlan. London: Sheed and Ward, 1930.

———. *Scholasticism and Politics*. Trans. by Mortimer J. Adler. New York: The Macmillan Co., no date.

May, Joseph. *The State and the Law of Christ*. Rome: Ponta Grossa, 1958.

Metz, Johannes Baptist, Ed. *Faith and the World of Politics*. New York, Paulist Press, 1968.

———. *Theology of the Word*. Trans. by William Glen-Doepel. New York: Herder and Herder, 1969.

Moody, Joseph N., Ed. *Church and Society: Catholic Social and Political Thought and Movements, 1789-1950*. New York: Arts, Inc., 1953.

———. *The Challenge of Mater et Magistra*. New York: Herder and Herder, 1963.

Mueller, Alois. *Obedience in the Church*. Trans. by Hilda Graef. Westminster, Maryland, Newman Press, 1966.

Murphy, Edward F., S.S.J., *St. Thomas' Political Doctrine and Democracy*. Washington, D.C.: Catholic University of America, 1931.

Murphy, Francis X. *Politics and the Early Christians*. New York: Desclee Company, Inc., 1967.

Murray, John Courtney, S.J. *The Problem of Religious Freedom*. Westminster, Maryland, Newman Press, 1965.

———. *Religious Liberty*. New York: Macmillan, 1966.

————. *We Hold These Truths*. Garden City, New York: Image Books, 1964.

Nagle, William J., Ed. *Morality and Modern War*. Baltimore, Helicon Press, 1960.

National Advisory Commission on Selective Service. *In Pursuit of Equity: Who Serves When Not All Serve?* Washington, D.C.: U.S. Government Printing Office, 1967.

Newman, Jeremiah. *Studies in Political Morality*. Dublin: Scepter, 1963.

O'Donnell, Charles P., Ed. *The Church in the World*. Milwaukee: The Bruce Publishing Co., 1967.

Osgood, Robert E. *Force, Order and Justice*. Baltimore: Johns Hopkins Press, 1967.

Paul VI. *Ecclesiam Suam*. London: Catholic Truth Society, 1965.

————. *Progressio Populorum*. Boston: Daughters of St. Paul, 1967.

Pius XII. *Selected Letters and Addresses of Pius XII*. London: The Catholic Truth Society, 1949.

Plamenatz, J. P. *Consent, Freedom and Political Obligation*. London: Oxford University Press, 1968.

Powers, Francis J., Ed. *Papal Pronouncements on the Political Order*. Westminster, Maryland: Newman Press, 1952.

Quigley, Thomas E., Ed. *American Catholics and Vietnam*. Grand Rapids, Michigan: W. B. Eirdman, 1968.

Rahner, Karl, S.J. *The Dynamic Element in the Church*. Trans. by W. J. O'Hara. New York: Herder and Herder, 1964.

————. *Obedience in the Church*. Washington, D.C.: Corpus Books, 1968.

———— and Herbert Vorgrimler. *Theological Dictionary*. Trans. by Richard Strachan. New York: Herder and Herder, 1965.

Ramsey, Paul. *War and the Christian Conscience*. Durham, North Carolina: Drake University Press, 1961.

————. *The Just War*. New York: Charles Scribner's Sons, 1968.

Rawls, John. *A Theory of Justice*. Cambridge: The Belknap Press of Harvard University Press, 1971.

Regan, Richard J., S.J. *American Pluralism and the Catholic Conscience*. New York: Macmillan, 1963.

Roberts, Archbishop, S.J. *Black Popes: Authority: Its Use and Abuse*. London: Longmans, Green and Co., 1954.

Rohr, John A. *Prophets Without Honor*. Nashville: Abingdon Press, 1971.

Rommen, Heinrich A. *The State in Catholic Thought: A Treatise in Political Philosophy*. St. Louis: B. Herder Book Co., 1945.

Ryan, John A. *The Catholic Church and the Citizen*. New York: Macmillan, 1928.

Ryan, John A. and Francis J. Boland. *Catholic Principles of Politics*.

New York: Macmillan, 1952.

Schillebeeckx, Edward, O.P. *God, The Future of Man*. Trans. by N. D. Smith. New York: Sheed and Ward, 1968.

Schlier, Heinrich. *The Relevance of the New Testament*. New York: Herder and Herder, 1968.

Sheppard, Vincent F. *Religion and the Concept of Democracy*. Washington, D.C.: Catholic University of America, 1949.

Stratmann, Francis, O.P. *War and Christianity Today*. Trans. by John Doebles. Westminster, Maryland: Newman Press, 1965.

Sturzo, Luigi. *Church and State*. Trans. by Barbara Carter. Notre Dame: University of Notre Dame Press, 1962.

Treoltsch, Ernst. *The Social Teachings of the Christian Churches*. Vols. 1-2. Trans. by Olive Wyon. New York: Harper Torchbook, 1960.

Tucker, Robert W. *Just War and Vatican Council II*. New York: Council on Religion and International Affairs, 1966.

United States Catholic Conference. *The Teachings of Pope Paul VI*. Washington D.C.: United States Catholic Conference Publishing Office, 1971.

Vorgrimler, Herbert, Ed. *Commentary on the Documents of Vatican II*. Vol. 5. Trans. by W. J. O'Hara. New York: Herder and Herder, 1969.

Walz, Kenneth N. *Man, the State, and War*. New York: Columbia University Press, 1959.

Walzer, Michael. *Obligations: Essays on Disobedience, War and Citizenship*. Cambridge: Harvard University Press, 1970.

Yates, Gerald F., Ed. *Papal Thought on the State*. New York: Appleton-Century-Crofts, Inc., 1958.

Yzermans, Vincent A., Ed. *The Major Addresses of Pope Pius XII*. Vols 1-2. St. Paul: North Central Publishing Co., 1961.

Zahn, Gordon C. *German Catholics and Hitler's Wars*. New York: Sheed and Ward, 1962.

———. *In Solitary Witness*. New York: Holt, Rinehart and Winston, 1964.

———. *War, Conscience and Dissent*. New York: Hawthorn Books, Inc., 1967.

Articles

Connally, Michael. "Pope Pius XII on Democracy." *Irish Monthly*, 73 (October, 1945), 407-17.

Connery, John R., S.J. "War, Conscience and the Law: The State of the Question." *Theological Studies*, 31 (June, 1970), 288-300.

Curran, Charles E. "Catholic Ethics Today in the Light of the Dialogue with Protestant Ethics." Presidential Address to the

American Society of Christian Ethics. 21 January 1972.

Egan, E. J. "Freedom and Authority in the Church: A Study of Recent Papal and Episcopal Statements." *The Catholic Worker* 23 (January, 1957), 1.

Ellis, John Tracey. "Church and State: An American Tradition." *Harper's Magazine,* 207 (November, 1953), 63-67.

Farraher, John J., S.J. "Notes on Moral Theology." *Theological Studies* 21 (December, 1960), 593.

————. "Moral Preemption: The Natural Law and Conscience-based Claims in Relation to Legitimate State Expectations." *Hastings Law Journal* 17 (1966), 439-51.

Harrington, Michael. "Moral Obligation and Political Opposition." *Worldview* (March, 1967), 6.

Hehir, Brian J. "The Idea of a Political Theology, 1." *Worldview* 16 (January, 1971), 5-7.

————. "The Idea of a Political Theology, 2." *Worldview* 16 (February, 1971), 5-7.

Lefever, Ernest W. "Patriotism and Religious Values." *Worldview* 1 (May, 1958), 3-5.

Lewy, Guenter. "Superior Orders, Nuclear Warfare, and the Dictates of Conscience: The Dilemma of Military Obedience in the Atomic Age." *American Political Science Review,* 55 (March, 1961), 3-23.

Love, Thomas T. "Roman Catholic Theories of 'Indirect Power'." *Journal of Church and State,* 9 (Winter, 1967), 71-85.

McCormick, Richard A., S.J. "Notes on Moral Theology." *Theological Studies,* 28 (June, 1967), 785-96.

————. "Notes on Moral Theology." *Theological Studies,* 27 (June, 1966), 633-38.

————. "Notes on Moral Theology." *Theological Studies,* 30 (December, 1969), 668-80.

Murray, John Courtney, S.J. "Governmental Repression of Heresy." *Proceedings* of the Catholic Theological Society of America, 3 (March, 1949), 42.

————. "The Problem of 'The Religion of the State'." *American Ecclesiastical Review,* 124 (May, 1951), 327-52.

————. "Contemporary Orientation of Catholic Theology in Church and State in the Light of History." *Cross Currents,* 2 (Fall, 1951), 15-55.

————. "Leo XIII on Church and State: The General Structure of the Controversy." *Theological Studies,* 14 (March, 1953), 1-30.

————. "Leo XIII: Separation of Church and State." *Theological Studies* 14 (June, 1953), 145-214.

————. "Leo XIII: Two Concepts of Government." *Theological*

Studies, 14 (December, 1953), 511-67.

⸻. "Leo XIII: Government and the Order of Culture." *Theological Studies,* 15 (March, 1954), 1-33.

⸻. "The Church and Totalitarian Democracy." *Theological Studies,* 14 (March, 1953), 523-63.

⸻. "The Issue of Church and State at Vatican Council II." *Theological Studies,* 27 (June, 1966), 580-606.

⸻. "The Problem of Religious Freedom." *Theological Studies,* 25 (December, 1964), 503-75.

⸻. "On the Structure of the Church-State Problem," in *The Catholic Church in World Affairs,* ed. by Waldemar Gurian and M. A. Fitzsimmons. (Notre Dame: The University of Notre Dame Press, 1954.)

Ottaviani, Cardinal. "Church and State: Some Present Problems in the Light of the Teaching of Pope Pius XII." *American Ecclesiastical Review,* 128 (May, 1953), 321-34.

Potter, Ralph. "Conscientious Objection to Particular Wars." in *Religion and the Public Order,* Vol. 4. Ed. by Donald A. Giannella (Ithaca: Cornell University Press, 1968).

Quade, Quentin L. "Civil Disobedience and the State." *Worldview,* 10 (November, 1967), 4-9.

Rabinove, S. "One War Yes, Another War No." *America,* 120 (31 May 1969), 647-68.

Rahner, Karl, S.J. "Reflection on Obedience: A Basic Ignatian Concept." *Cross Currents,* 10 (Fall, 1960), 363-74.

Ramsey, Paul. "Selective Conscientious Objection: Warrants and Reservations," in *A Conflict of Loyalties,* ed. by James Finn (New York: Pegasus, 1968).

Rohr, John. "Just Wars and Selective Objectors." *Review of Politics,* (April, 1971), 185-201.

Sibley, Mulford. "On Political Obligation and Civil Disobedience." *Journal* of the Minnesota Academy of Science, 33 (1965), 67-72.

Springer, Robert H., S.J. "Notes on Moral Theology." *Theological Studies,* 30 (June, 1969), 249-88.

Zahn, Gordon C. "National Loyalty and Religious Values." *Worldview,* 7 (July-August, 1964), 4-7.

⸻. "The Test of the 'Just War'." *Worldview,* 8 (December, 1965), 10-13.

⸻. "An Explosive Principle." *Worldview,* 10 (March, 1967), 6-8.